WHISPERS FROM GOD

Daily Devotionals For Women

VICTORIA M. HOWARD

authorHOUSE®

AuthorHouse™
1663 Liberty Drive
Bloomington, IN 47403
www.authorhouse.com
Phone: 1 (800) 839-8640

Published by AuthorHouse 11/30/2019

ISBN: 978-1-7283-3773-9 (sc)
ISBN: 978-1-7283-3774-6 (hc)
ISBN: 978-1-7283-3775-3 (e)

Print information available on the last page.

Preface

WHISPERS FROM GOD is a book for everyone. It's for believers, those sitting on the fence unsure of which way to go, and for the ones living in the dark seeking spiritual direction.

There's a devotional or inspirational saying for every day of the year. Some are **Whispers from God,** while others are themes or passages from the Bible to help guide you in your walk with Jesus Christ.

These devotions may be someone's only Bible or chance to hear the Word for they find it difficult in understanding the Holy Book.

Inspiration is subjective, as different people will find different things to be inspiring. However, children of God can unite around one inspirational source—God Himself.

God is the foundation for all of our inspirations because He is the basis for all good things and everything worth imitating.

When you wake up in the morning and have that first cup of coffee, open **Whispers From God** and read the devotion of the day. Turn off the television or radio and make sure it is quiet. This is your 'One-On-One' time with the Lord.

Read it slowly, letting the message resonate into your mind and soul. Hopefully, it will feed you the nourishment and substance that's essential in order to live in His presence so He may bless you with peace and everlasting measure.

What better way to start the day than with your creator, protector, and best friend Jesus Christ by your side, for He is omnipotent, omnipresent and omniscient. May He bless you with His peace and love.

Introduction

As I sit with pen in hand, my life flashes in front of me. Decades of happy, sad, and transcendental experiences appear in my head.

It is said that when a person is confronted with a Near-Death

Experience certain events that have been lying dormant in the back of their mind start to materialize-- like a movie playing in slow motion.

One day we will all have a day of personal reckoning—when we are called to account for our actions, sins, and our eyes are opened to our past mistakes or misdeeds.

For me that day came on May 1, 2018 when I was beset with a health situation that literally knocked me off my horse and changed my life forever.

Many people have said I've been blessed with a colorful, exciting life. Having been a model, dancer, and beauty queen, opened doors to a world of the rich and famous. I partied with movie stars and was the guest on a yacht of the owner of one of the world's largest beauty and cosmetic company.

But in reality it was all a mere illusion, a euphoric high, leaving me with an empty void inside. The enemy (Satan) relentlessly tempted me through things I knew as familiar and stimulating---- specifically money, fame and men.

Then one day I stepped out of my comfort zone and tried something I had never attempted before—I wrote a book. Over the next decade I penned dozens of books on relationships, equine related, self-help, biographies, and children's books.

Whispers From God is by far my favorite for I had the best co-author by my side inspiring and guiding me.

Several of my books were recognized in magazines and television--- one even received a literary award. Although my work was acknowledged--- not one made the 'best seller' list—or even came close.

One day I decided to write a novel---the type of book that was selling and people bought. It was a fictional story about sex, gay marriage, and the lustful temptations of the world--- things not taught in the Bible.

As I was writing, I felt a tinge of quilt and shame. I had this gnawing feeling I was doing something God didn't approve of. After all, I was supposed to be a Christian--- a child of God--- so how could I bring myself to educate people on these taboos and sins?

Immediately the book received national attention. It was even spotlighted in The New York Times, so I hired a publicist from Hollywood to help promote it.

I appeared on television shows in Tampa, Florida, and Los Angeles, California. I was introduced to the mother of an actor who loved the book and wanted to turn it into a movie.

I couldn't believe it! My book was finally going to make it big. All those years of sitting over the computer would finally pay off.

And then---------BOOM! Several mornings after returning from the west coast I woke in a cold sweat at 3 a.m. gasping for air. I passed it off as an anxiety attack and ignored it.

The next morning I was woken again with a heavy tightness in my chest and told my son, "I think it's time we go to the hospital."

In the emergency room I was diagnosed with having a double saddle pulmonary embolism in my lungs. The doctor said one clot was massive and my chance of survival was 50/50.

I underwent a procedure to dissolve the thrombosis and was put on a blood thinner.

The next three days I spent in ICU and underwent a second operation to implant a small metal device called an IVC Cava Filter. It is designed to catch any clots before they traveled to my lungs or heart, for the doctor said I still had a clot in the bottom of my leg.

This all happened so quickly. One day I was on top of the world and the next day I was at death's door.

Looking back, I believe this was God way of chastening me for writing something that did not honor Him! I was frightened and began to really examine my life.

I searched my soul to contemplate what He was trying to tell me.

At that time a good friend had given me a book written by Sarah Young called *Jesus Calling.* As I began reading, my fear began to dissipate. I felt an overwhelming presence of peace and love. The messages I received addressed what I had been seeking all my life--- a deeper experience of Jesus' presence and peace.

The health scare was a wake-up call! I prayed and prayed about it and asked God what He was trying to tell me.

That night I was awoken with a message. They were '*Whispers from God*'. I knew I was to write a book—a book that was comprised of inspirational sayings and devotionals.

As I began meditating on God, certain days I received messages, so I kept a pad and pen with me to jot them down.

Then there were were days I heard nothing, but enjoyed my time in really getting to know Him. Other times I experienced a "fullness of joy" in His presence (Psalm 16:11), or simply enjoyed His company and peace.

There were days I was enlightened with the most beautiful messages from my Father.

I wanted to share these messages with you. You will notice that some are written in the first person singular (I, Me) which are referring to Christ.

Although most of the whispers are geared towards women, men can also read, contemplate, and practice these messages, for we are all one.

I knew I was ready to embark on the biggest journey of my life--- a spiritual quest--- so I enrolled in a Bible College. After intense studying I was ordained a minister and received a Doctorate in Divinity.

This is totally opposite of what my life had been up until then: money, glamour and the worldly things. But I have never been happier, and I discovered that NO--- money DOES NOT buy the real happiness we all desperately seek.

I am sure my health scare was God's way of slowing me down--- showing me what was really important, but I often asked, *"God couldn't you have picked something a little less harsh?"*

It has been quite a journey and the fact I am mortal and of the flesh, I am occasionally confronted with trials and tribulations. As I grow closer to God, the enemy tries harder to intervene, but during these times I remember Psalm 46:10: *"Be still and know that I am God." (NIV)*

Whispers From God contains a message or special saying for each day and a Scriptural reference, psalm, or proverb that correlates to it.

Hopefully these **Whispers from God** will inspire people along their journey in life to honor God, our Father. I am not the author---I only held the pen.

I hope this book guides you down the correct path to living a content life, have a relationship with God, and prepares you for the ultimate finale--- an eternal life with Jesus Christ—our Lord and Savior.

Victoria

Dedication

I dedicate ***Whispers From God*** to my Lord and Savior, Jesus Christ. He is the only one who has never left or deceived me.

Also, this book is for my sisters and brothers in Christ who have helped me along my walk with the Lord: *My sister Karen, Cousins Ron, Billy, and Gloria. My daughter-in-law Kristine, and my dear friends Coleen, Lyndell, Ruth, and Wes.*

And last but not least, I dedicate this book to my first unborn grandchild, Vivian Grace, who is due April 2020. Thank you, God for answering my prayers and blessing me once again.

JANUARY

January 1

FOCUS ON THE FUTURE

Today is the first day of a new year. Give thanks to me for giving you the ultimate gift of life. Learn how to program yourself on focusing what I have planned for you. Rid yourself of any thoughts and regrets you may have of your past.

Holding onto the past is like wearing a two-ton weight around your neck. It weighs you down and immobilizes you from moving on.

During your life unexpected events will arise which will test your faith. Respond to them calmly---never forgetting that I am with you.

Trust in me in everything you do and I shall lead you down the right path.

Philippians 3:12 *"Not that I have already attained, or am already perfected: but I press on, that I may lay hold of that for which Christ Jesus has also laid hold of me."* (NKJV)

January 2

DO NOT WORRY

Relax and have faith in my healing presence, instead of letting your mind fret over unresolved situations and problems that arise.

Close your eyes and allow me to enter. The light of my presence is the only answer to peace.

I will be your rock and anchor. There is nothing I cannot fix, but you must have faith in me. Instead of allowing difficult situations to draw you into worrying, try to view them as preparing you for my glorious intervention. Keep your eyes open to what I am doing in your life.

Worrying is a sin and I am knocking on the door. Cast your worries aside, open the door and let me in.

Matthew 6:27 *And which of you by being anxious can add a single hour to his span of life? (ESV)*

January 3

LET GO AND LET GOD

Should haves, could haves and would haves are something we've all said in our life. We are human and all make mistakes—but at the time it seemed like we were doing the right thing.

You must learn to "let it go" and not dwell on the choices you have made. If it were possible to go back and rewind the situation, we all would. To keep going over and over about something you cannot change is senseless. It is like a broken record that can replay over and over again. Take that record off the player and put it on the shelf never to pick it up again.

Life is about learning, and mistakes are merely lessons we needed to learn.

I am a non-judging God and will not judge you, for I'm not a cold-hearted God. When I chasten and discipline you it is so you will turn to me. My discipline is only a response of my love and desire for each of you to be holy.

Ephesians 4:32 *Be kind and compassionate to one another, forgiving each other, just as Christ God forgave you. (NIV)*

January 4

MY GIFTS TO YOU

Take time to enjoy the precious gifts I have given you: The sunshine, the flowers, the animals, your family and friends. These presents are all meant to be pointers to me---the creator of all.

Seek to live in my unconditional love and surround yourself with my light that always protects you.

I have loved you my child, with an undying love. If you have faith in me, I will lead you to peace and happiness. What I will give you cannot be bought with money. By pointing you in the right direction I prepare each and every day for you. Cling to my hand and enjoy peace in my presence.

John 3:16 *For God so loved the world that he gave his only Son, that whoever believes in him should not perish, but have eternal life. (NIV)*

January 5

A WINNING TEAM

Problems and unexpected situations keep surfacing in your life: Financial matters, health situations and family trouble. You question me as to why these things are happening to you.

Instead of questioning me, thank Me for them.

Not focusing on the negative allows the problem to become insignificant and lose its power.

Together as a team we can deal with any problem—no matter how big or small. Most of these situations are really pointless--- simply borrowed from tomorrow.

Rest assured, I will take this problem out of today and store it somewhere in the distant future. In return I will give you a feeling of peace and calmness that can only come from my presence.

Proverbs 3:5 *Trust in the Lord with all your heart and lean not on your own understanding. In all your ways acknowledge Him, and He shall direct your path. (NIV)*

January 6

A STOP ALONG THE WAY

Don't get caught up in the world and the things in it. This is just a temporary stop along your journey back home. You may live 30, 40, 50, 60 or more years before you return to me. I want you to live each day as if it were your last—because it just might be.

I am the only one who knows when you will be called home and in what way. I knew it before you were ever born. No matter how good you take care of yourself there is no avoiding death. Nobody gets out alive.

You make plans for the future while I sit here with a grin, for it is not up to you. Nobody has ever lived forever and nobody ever will.

I have given you the gift of life to experience the precious things I have created and to honor me, and when your time is up you will return to me and spend eternity in perfect bliss and joy.

Proverbs 3:1 *My child, never forget the things I have taught you. Store my commands in your heart. If you do this, you will live many years and your life will be satisfying. (NLT)*

January 7

TRUST IN ME

Trust in ME—not in your friends, family, money, or worldly things. They will all let you down, but I will never leave you.

Your mind often plays games and leads you down dark alleys. You must go deep inside to pull your faith out and believe that no matter what the income of your situation is, it will be okay. After all, I am in control and will never let one of my children down.

No matter what circumstance you are experiencing now--- know I am there with you.

I may chastise or chase you, but it is for your own good. Remember, the only way to show true love is for a parent to discipline their child when they do wrong. I love you and know what is best for you.

Revelation 21:4 *He will wipe every tear from their eyes and there will be no more death or sorrow or crying or pain. All these things are gone forever. (NLT)*

January 8

THE TONGUE IS A SWORD

Anger, rage, and losing your temper are very distinctive emotions and a waste of energy. This reveals a lack of faith that God loves you and is in control. Whenever someone upsets you, take a deep breath before saying something that you will later be sorry for.

Words have meaning and can bring joy and admonishment, but they can also leave deep wounds, where scars cannot be seen or easily healed. Verbal abuse is as bad as physical abuse.

The tongue can be hurtful and evil—full of deadly poison. Think before you speak, for once the words come out you cannot take them back. The uncontrolled tongue is especially harmful and dangerous to the body of Christ.

The next time you are about to say something you will be sorry for, take a deep breath and pray. It will save you a lot of grief and pain and stop you from saying something you can never take back.

Psalm 37:9 *For the evildoers shall be cut off, but those who wait for the Lord shall inherit the land. (ESV)*

January 9

TURN THE OTHER CHEEK

As hard as it may be, when someone wrongs you, do what Jesus did and turn your cheek. Evil rules the world and every day we are tempted to stray by things that may not seem at the time to be wrong, but in the end we may pay the price.

Evil is real and prevalent in the world today. But you must remember that God ordains all things that come to pass—including evil.

In the Bible it says, *"Let no one say when he is tempted. I am being tempted by God, for God cannot be tempted with evil, and he attempts no one."* James 1:13 *(KJV)*

The next time someone says something that hurts you--- stop, take a deep breath and pray. God will strengthen you and ease the pain.

Psalm 37:27 *Turn from evil and do good and you will live in the land forever. For the Lord loves justice and He will never abandon the godly. (NLT)*

January 10

BEWARE OF WOLVES IN SHEEP CLOTHING

When we take that first step in obeying God, we will discover that He is good and kind. Do not be deceived by those who come dressed in sheep's clothing. They are merely wolves that work on your kindness and naivety. The world is filled with wolves in sheep clothing. Beware of your surroundings and those who come into your life.

Obedience is an essential part of the Christian faith. It is defined as "Dutiful or submissive compliance to the commands of one on authority."

Dutiful means it is our obligation to obey God, just as Jesus fulfilled His duty to the Father by dying on the cross for our sins.

When a child is obedient to his parent, it shows respect and love. We must be obedient to God our Father and we will be rewarded.

Psalm 34: 8 *Taste and see that the Lord is good. Oh, the joys of those who take refuge in him! Fear the Lord, you his Godly people, for those who fear him will have all they need. Even strong young lions sometimes go hungry, but those who trust in the Lord will lack no good thing. (NLT)*

January 11

I AM HOLDING YOUR HAND

Life can be hard for we live in a fallen world. This was not God's plan for He wanted us to be happy and live in peace and harmony, but because of the original sin executed by our first parents, Adam and Eve in the Garden of Eden, there is pain, sickness and disease in the world.

Many times you go through something and feel like you are all alone. You may think that nobody cares. All you want is someone to put their arms around you and tell you everything will be okay, but you find yourself alone to face whatever it is you are going through.

But remember, you are NOT alone, for Jesus is right beside you. He will never leave you. Although you can't see Him, be still and know He is there, holding your hand.

Isaiah 41: 10-14 *Don't be afraid, for I am with you. Don't be discouraged, for I am your God. I will strengthen you and help you. I will hold you up with my victorious right hand. (NLT)*

January 12

CALL OUT MY NAME

Whenever you feel distant from me, close your eyes and whisper My name. Reach out and be aware of My Presence.

I can hear you and when you call out to me, it is music to my ears. You just have to ask and you will receive.

Feel my arms wrap around you as I ease your pain. Every day set aside five minutes and make it, "our time." You don't have to see me to know I am there for I am your best friend, your savior, your father, and will never leave you.

John 16:23 *At that time you won't need to ask me for anything. I tell you the truth, you will ask the Father directly, and He will grant your request because you use my name. (NLT)*

January 13

LAUGHTER IS THE BEST MEDICINE

Learn to enjoy each day, relax and appreciate the life I have given you. Try not to take your circumstances so seriously. Laughter is the best medicine and will help lighten your load.

I knew exactly what I was doing when I created laughter.

Humor and joy are mentioned many times throughout Scripture.

Laughter is powerful medicine. Laughter is a response to my tremendous love and grace that I shower on you.

Stop trying to carry the load of the world on your shoulders alone. Friends are one of my greatest gifts but do not rely strictly on them, for many will let you down.

I am your best friend and will never leave or deceive you.

Proverbs 17:17 *A friend loves at all times, and a brother is born for a time of adversity.* (NIV)

January 14

TRUST IN ME

Many people spend a fortune and countless years looking for someone who understands them. Look no further. I am the only one who knows the intimacies of your heart, mind, and spirit. I know everything about you. I even know how many hairs there are on your head.

Have faith and trust in Me and your life will be more peaceful and fulfilled. Total trust is the one thing I demand from you.

It's funny how you can trust a friend, a lover, the stock market, even someone you hardly know; yet you have trouble trusting Me.

Without trust in Me, your life will be filled with anxiety, depression and uncertainty. Trusting in Me will transform your life and bring the peace you have been seeking.

Proverbs 3:5 *Trust in the Lord with all your heart and lean not on your own understanding. In all your ways acknowledge Him and He shall direct your path. (NKJV)*

◆ January 15 ◆

LIVING IN A FALLEN WORLD

The world we live in is a fallen one. In order to get through each day you need someone who is going to hold your hand as you walk through your problems and pain.

That someone is Me. I did not make the world to be full of sin and corruption, but unfortunately Adam and Eve destroyed that perfect world.

Do not hate them, for this was the way it was meant to be. You have a choice of doing right from wrong and to make your life on earth a blessed one.

*****

*** As disciples of the Lord Jesus Christ, we want to live well and effectively for Him. But how can we do so? As followers of Christ we can gain insight into these issues by considering the life of the Lord Jesus---the perfect example. How do we live for Christ? We do it by prayer, following his teachings, loving our neighbors and reading the Bible.

Romans 8:28 *And we know that God causes everything to work together for the good of those who love him and are called according to his purpose. (NLT)*

January 16

PRACTICE THE 3 'L'S

Listen, Learn, Laugh. These are the 3 things you must do if you want a life that is full of peace and joy.

1) **Listen** to what I say to you.
   How do you do that? By being quiet and still.

2) **Learn** what I teach you by getting in the Bible and reading my scriptures.
3) **Laugh**. Laughter is the best medicine for the soul.
   By practicing these three things daily you will please me for you are obeying my commands.

Just like the 3 monkeys who are a pictorial maxim embodying the proverbial principle: See No Evil, Hear No Evil and Speak No Evil. Be wise and listen, think before you speak, and steer away from anything evil. By practicing these three things you will find your life is more peaceful and happy.

Exodus 20:6 *And showing mercy unto thousands of them that love me, and keep my commandments. (KJV)*

January 17

I AM THE GLUE

Do you feel like you are coming apart at the seams and you can't see light at the end of the tunnel? Do you feel like you are a chicken without a head going around and around and around?

Fear no longer for I am the glue you need. I will secure your life and give you the peace you seek. I am that brilliant light that is and will always be at the end of the tunnel. For the light will lead you back home to Heaven.

Keep walking with me along the path I have chosen for you. Everyone has a unique, separate path. I am there with each and every one of you. Your reward will be living eternal life with me in Heaven.

Psalm 37:23 *The Lord directs the steps of the Godly. He delights in every detail of their lives. Though they stumble, they will never fall, for the Lord holds them with his hand. (NLT)*

January 18

PRIDE: ONE OF THE SEVEN CAPITAL SINS

What is pride? Pride is a feeling, deep pleasure, or satisfaction derived from ones' own achievements--- the achievements of those with whom one is closely associated with, or from qualities or possessions that are widely admired.

Pride is a sin. There is nothing wrong with being happy that you have accomplished your goals, but you should be thankful that I gave you that ability.

I am the one who enables you to excel in any activity. Pride is giving yourself the credit for something that I have already accomplished. Pride is taking the glory that belongs to me alone and giving it to yourself.

Anything that we accomplish would not have been possible were it not for Me enabling and sustaining you.

Proverbs 29:23 *A man's pride shall bring him low because it subjects him to the imputation of folly. (KJV)*

January 19

YOU GOTTA HAVE FAITH

Faith is the confirmation of things we do not see and the conviction of their reality--- perceiving a real fact that is not revealed to the senses.

Faith is a word that is difficult to tie down to one meaning. It is the evidence of things not seen and believing in something because your life experiences have proven it to you.

Faith is the backbone of Christianity. The Bible tells us that faith is *"Being sure of what we hope for and certain of what we do not see." Hebrews 11:1 (NIV)*

According to the Bible, faith is belief in the one, true God without actually seeing Him. Faith is a gift from God-- not because we deserve it, have earned it, or are worthy of it. It is a precious endowment from the Lord. Without faith we cannot have eternal life in Heaven with Jesus Christ.

Hebrews 11:1 *Now faith is the substance of things hoped for, for the evidence of things not seen. (KJV)*

January 20

BE STILL

Bring to Me the sacrifice of your time. In this hectic world, everyone is busy trying to make a dollar or to impress someone. Take time out of your day and sit quietly in My Presence.

I will calm your soul and bestow blessings, for I am pleased by our time together. Enjoy our 'one on one' time today.

Time management is important because of the brevity of your life. Our earthly sojourn is significantly shorter than we are inclined to think.

Regarding our work ethic, remember that I did all my work in six days and rested on the seventh. It should be noted that rest is a legitimate and needed use of time.

Most importantly, we need to schedule regular, daily time together, for it is I who equips you to carry out the tasks I have given you.

Psalm 103: *Let all that I am praise the Lord; with my whole heart, I will praise his holy name. Let all that I am praise the Lord: may I never forget the good things he does for me. (NLT)*

January 21

IT'S YOUR BIRTHDAY

Birthdays are something many people fret about for it means they are one year older. Instead of looking at it negatively, know that you are one day closer to being in total peace, love, and bliss with God in Heaven.

Do not be content to settle down in a rocking chair and just wait for your Heavenly Father to call you home. Do you look back on your youth and recall the plans you made, the dreams you had, the mountains you were going to climb, and think that it didn't happen?

God had something good planned for you. Trust in Him and wait. Life isn't over yet.

Philippians 1:6 *Being confident of this very thing, that he which hath begun a good work in you will perform it until the day of Christ Jesus. (KJV)*

January 22

LET THE LITTLE CHILDREN COME TO ME

Children are a blessing in our lives and very important. They are a valuable part of God's Kingdom. God created the family. His design was for a man and a woman to marry for life and raise children to know and honor Him.

In the Bible God says, *"Bring them up in the discipline and instruction of the Lord."* As parents we should train our children as God trains us. *"Slow to anger."* (Numbers 14:18) *(KJV)*

The word 'discipline' comes from the root word *disciple.* To discipline means to make a disciple. The goal to good parenting is to produce wise children who know and honor God with their lives.

"Behold, children are a heritage from the Lord, the fruit of the womb a reward."(ESV) (Psalm 127:3)

Praise and support your children and teach them to love the Lord.

Proverbs 20:7 *The Godly walk with integrity; blessed are their children who follow them. (NLT)*

January 23

LOVE YOUR NEIGHBOR AS YOURSELF

It is said there is a thin line between love and hate. Do you love someone, but really don't like him? Hate and love are two very strong emotions.

When you love someone it is easy and feels right, but when you hate or strongly dislike him, it may start out small but grows as it is fed. It is like a cancer that eats away inside of you. It holds you back from the joy and peace you desire.

Loving your neighbor is not as hard as it looks. It simply means respecting others.

It takes as much energy to hate as is does to love, so is it really worth it holding on to a grudge? Whenever you feel ill towards someone, pray to Me for this feeling to leave. If you pray, you can't hate because you can't do two things at the same time.

1 John 4:20 *Whoever claims to love God yet hates a brother or sister is a liar. For whoever does not love their brother and sister, whom they have seen, cannot love God, whom they have not seen. (NIV)*

January 24

FREINDSHIP

Friends are one of the greatest gifts you will ever receive from me. Friendships can come in layers. There are casual friendships, which can be people you work with on a daily basis, and then there are "real" friends.

Our lives can be strongly influenced by the friends we have. That is why we must be able to identify who are our true friends.

In your lifetime if you have 1 or 2 really good friends, you are blessed beyond your wildest dreams.

These are people with who you share the depths of your soul and who care about what you are doing and feeling. They are rock solid and will always be there for you—in the good times and bad.

True friends are a gift from me, so be thankful and tell them how much you love them.

John 15:13 *Greater love has no one than this: to lay down one's life for one's friends. (NIV)*

January 25

A COMPASSIONATE FATHER

Today we live in a culture that tries to minimize the role of a father. Turn on the television and in many cases the father is viewed as the comic relief of the show.

The Bible is clear that Fathers are to be spiritual leaders in the home. Our earthly father was chosen for us by God, before we were born.

The compassionate father will extend patience while his children learn the basics.

We are to always love and respect our earthly father as we do our Heavenly one. A good father makes all the difference in a child's life. He's a pillar of strength, support, and discipline.

The position and authority of the father are expressly assumed and sanctioned in Scripture, as a likeness of that of the Almighty over his creatures.

Always treat your father with respect and show him love.

Ephesians 6:2 *Honor thy father and the mother; which is the first commandment with promise. (KJV)*

January 26

SATAN ATTACKS WHEN YOU ARE AT YOUR WEAKEST

Learning to trust in God is a journey. The journey will not always be an easy one for the enemy will be lurking and waiting for an opportunity to lead you down the wrong path.

He does this by telling lies, and convincing you that you are worthless and not worthy of God's love.

Satan acts when we are weak. Stay strong and know that you ARE worthy, for God loves you unconditionally. He created you just the way He wanted you to be.

When the devil tempts you through worldly things such as lust, sex, money, and fame, tell him, "The Lord rebukes you Satan in the name of Christ Jesus." Then continue down the path of light knowing Jesus is holding you with his right hand.

Isaiah 26:3 *You will keep in perfect peace those whose minds are steadfast, because they trust in you. (NIV)*

January 27

EVEN PEOPLE IN THE BIBLE WERE LONELY

Do you know someone who feels unwanted and alone? There is nothing worse than to feel like nobody loves or wants you.

Sometimes people just need words of wisdom or a simple hug to let them know you care.

People who feel this way believe they have no purpose for getting up in the morning. They feel invisible and that there is no reason to go on living.

Sadly, there are many people in the world who feel like this. Be God's hands, voice and heart, and reach out and touch them. Let them know there is someone who cares. There are many people in the world who are in a hospital and have no one to visit them. Be a volunteer and show them someone cares.

Make a difference in the world and be a child of God.

Romans 12:4-5 *Just as each of us has one body with many members and these members do not all have the same function, so in Christ we, though many, form one body, and each member belongs to all the others. (BSB)*

January 28

WORRYING IS A SIN

If worry were a gift, I would be spiritually blessed for I am the worrywart of the century. Ever since I was a child, I worried about what if something happens, what could happen, and what if it doesn't happen.

I know worrying is a sin and as hard as I tried, the evil one kept putting thoughts in my mind about things I had no control over.

It took me awhile but I learned how to defeat him in times like this. Whenever I start to worry---I pray. You cannot do two things at the same time, so when I start to worry I ask God's forgiveness for worrying and pray.

Then I give Him thanks for everything and my worries disappear.

Philippians 4:6 *Do not be anxious about anything, but in every situation, by prayer and petition with thanksgiving, present your requests to God. (NIV)*

January 29

BE STILL AND LISTEN

"Be still and listen." That is what God preaches us to do. Communication is the key to successful relationships. Communication is a two-way conversation.

How do we communicate with God? By praying.

When something weighs heavy on your heart, automatically bring it to God. You must learn to "Be still and listen" and see if He has something to say to you. He will answer you.

Choose the same time every day when you shut off the phone, television, and radio, and bring your problems, questions, and worries to the only one who can help---our Lord and Savior, Jesus Christ.

Psalm 46:10 *He says, "Be still and know that I am God; I will be exalted among the nations, I will be exalted in the earth."* (NIV)

January 30

LET THERE BE LIGHT

Most children are afraid of the dark. There are even some adults that have to sleep with a nightlight or television on, afraid of what lurks in the dark.

But there is also a darkness that is not caused by the lack of light. This darkness can be caused by job loss, illness, a broken marriage, or sin.

Do not worry, for you are never alone. God is always there by your side, helping you through this temporary difficult time. Have faith, trust, and remember, "This too shall pass."

What does the Bible say about how darkness appeared in the beginning? It states, *"In the beginning, God created the heavens and earth. The earth was without form and void and darkness was over the face of the deep."*

God made light—the rising and setting of the sun. The distinction between light and darkness is only from a human perspective and were created by God for the benefit of humanity from that perspective.

Do not be afraid of the dark, for there is light at the end of the tunnel. His name is Jesus Christ.

Job 11:18 *You will be secure because there is hope; you will look about you and take your rest in safety. (NIV)*

January 31

COMPASSION

What is compassion? It is a wonderful trait that many people unfortunately lack. It is the sympathetic consciousness of others' distress-- together with a desire to alleviate it. Compassion alludes to kindness and sympathy, but goes much deeper.

In the Bible 'compassion' means to have mercy, to feel sympathy, and to have pity.

We know that God is a compassionate and gracious God—slow to anger and quick to forgive-- abounding in love and faithfulness. His compassions never fail.

We are to be compassionate to others as God is to us. Love one another with brotherly affection. Outdo one another in showing honor. (Romans 12:10 *Be devoted to one another in love.)*

Ephesians 4:32 *Be kind to one another, tenderhearted, forgiving one another, as God in Christ forgave you. (KJV)*

FEBRUARY

February 1

YOU ARE ONLY HUMAN

It's all right to be human. Your mind will wander from time to time, taking you down the path of destruction. Do not be concerned, for I am with you—always.

As you live in close contact with Me, the light of My presence filters through you to bless others. You are human and your weakness is a wound that lets the Light of my Glory shine through. My strength and power show themselves most effective in your weakness.

I created you in My image, so you need not worry, for I am perfect. I came to earth as a human to take away all your sins and suffered for you. But I am also God the Father, the only one who is omnipotent and omnipresent.

Because you were created by Me in My image, you have nothing to worry about. Have faith and know I AM.

Colossians 2:6-7 *So then, just as you received Christ Jesus as Lord, continue to live our lives in Him, rooted and built up in him, rooted and built up in Him, strengthened in the faith as you were taught and overflowing with thankfulness. (KJV)*

February 2

CHANGE IS GOOD

Change is hard and at times scary, but it is necessary. Think back on your life and the changes you have gone through. Did they result in good growth? If there has been no change in your life, maybe it's about time there is.

If you don't take the step, you may find yourself in a rut---doing things the same way over and over again, only to end with the same result.

Change is a thing, not a person; as such, it's not good or bad. Things are simply things. If the change is good or bad, depends on the person who sees the change.

Ask God to help you embrace change. He will guide through what He wants you to do, no matter what your circumstances are.

Psalm 59:9-10 *You are my strength, I watch for you, for you, O God are my fortress, my God on whom I can rely. (NIV)*

February 3

TAKE A CHANCE

Same old, same old. Do you feel that everyone else is doing new and exciting things, but you are stuck in the same old rut?

It could be your fault, for you are so cautious that you are not willing to take a chance and take the leap to try something new.

Life is not static. It's always changing, so if you're not willing to make a change, you will be left doing the same thing in the same place, getting the same result.

Learn a new skill, take a class and take dance lessons. Volunteer for the refugee ministry in your church.

Yes, it will be a process to learn, but as long as you learn, from day to day you will grow and change.

You will never know what God has planned for you or where he is leading you if you aren't willing to explore a new path.

James 4:17 *If anyone, then, knows the good they ought to do and doesn't do it, it is sin for them. (NIV)*

February 4

I AM YOUR BFF

I am your best friend, as well as your creator and King. I'll always walk hand in hand with you through all your trials, tribulations, and daily activities.

Even in the darkest moments I will bring you light and peace and out of adversity.

My friendship is sincere and unconditional. There is no other friend like me!

John 15:13 says, "*Greater love has no one than this, that someone lay down his life for his friends.*" (KJV)

I have already befriended you. I will tell you your faults and follies and assist you with My hand and heart in times of adversity.

I am not a fair-weather friend like many of your human friends, for I will never abandon you. I know all your secrets and will never betray your trust.

Isaiah 61:3 *The Spirit of the Lord God is upon me; because the Lord hath appointed me to preach good tidings unto the meek; he hath sent me to bind up the brokenhearted. (NIV)*

February 5

CLEANSED WITH MY BLOOD

I am around, hovering over you, even as you seek my face. I am closer than you know. If my children could only recognize my Presence, they would never feel lonely.

Deep inside most of you have some awareness of My Presence, but many will run away and deny my existence, for my closeness frightens them.

Sin is a thought, attitude, action, or inaction, contrary to my will. My blood will cleanse all your sins.

My children have nothing to fear, for they are cleansed with My blood and clothed in My righteousness. Be blessed by My intimacy since I live inside you, guarding and protecting you.

Psalm 139:1 *Oh Lord, thou hast searched me and known me. (NIV)*

February 6

LAUGHTER IS THE BEST MEDICINE

Laughter is the best medicine. Learn to laugh at yourself and do not take your circumstances or yourself so harshly. Relax, and know that I, God, am with you.

Laughter is a physical reaction in humans consisting typically of rhythmical, often audible contractions of the diaphragm.

Laughter lightens up your load and lifts your heart and spirit. Your laughter rises to Heaven and pleases Me--- just as earthly parents delight in the laughter of their children, so I delight in hearing my children laugh.

Do not carry the weight of this troubled world on your shoulders. Instead, take My yoke upon you and learn from Me.

***Proverbs* 17:22** *A cheerful heart is good medicine but a crushed spirit dries up the bones. (NIV)*

February 7

ALL THINGS WORK FOR THE GOOD WHO LOVE ME

When you open your eyes in the morning, before you get out of bed, thank me for everything. No matter what your circumstances are at the time, remember that everything that is happening to you is supposed to happen, and for the best.

You are my child who I love very much and would never lead you astray or endanger you. At times you may wonder why you are going through something difficult; whether it be financial, personal, or health related. Remember, all things work for good to those that love Me.

Every day you wake up say, "I will trust you today, no matter what may come my way for I know that all things happen for a reason."

Romans 8:28 *And we know that in all things God works for the good of those who love Him, who have been called according to his purpose. (NIV)*

February 8

THIS TOO SHALL PASS

Feeling alone? Does it feel like the weight of the world is on your shoulders? Your inner calm and peace in My presence need not be shaken by what is going on around you.

You are living in a world that is filled with pain, anger and hatred. When you start to feel stressed, break away from the chains that bind you. Relax and remember that these circumstances, too, shall pass.

Do not let your heart be troubled and do not be afraid. The peace I give is sufficient to you.

All things—good and bad---- are only temporary. I promise you that you will get through whatever it is, for I am your Father and love you.

Proverbs 16:9 *In their hearts humans plan their course, but the Lord establishes their steps. (NIV)*

February 9

YOU CAN WORSHIP ANYWHERE

What does the Bible say about worship? Is it singing, clapping and/or raising your hands at church? Yes, worship is singing, but not only singing biblically--- it is a part of worship. It's about reverence and having a biblical fear of the Lord.

If worship is about humbling yourself before God, we have to consider the place of our feelings. People can fervently praise God with their mouths and still be far away from Him.

Remember, Jesus, is the perfect worshipper. In His incarnation He obeyed every commandment of God without flaw or failure.

As a born-again Christian, you can worship God in private—on your couch, reading your Bible, or singing praise in church. With the Holy Spirit inside of you, you can worship God anywhere at all.

Exodus 23:25 *Worship the Lord your God, and His blessing will be on your food and water. I will take away sickness from among you. (NIV)*

February 10

WORRYING IS A SIN

We worry about school, jobs, budgets, and relationships. We fret about our bills, financing, rising living expenses, and health issues.

Over the span of a lifetime, worry can add up to hours of valuable time that we can never get back. With that in mind, try to spend your time wisely and enjoyably.

The Bible says that worry accomplishes nothing. It teaches us that Christians are not to worry. Worrying won't solve a problem or bring about a possible solution—so why waste your time and energy on it?

Give your worries to God. There is no worry too big or too small for Him. When we give God our problems, He promises to give us the peace that transcends all understanding.

Matthew 6:27-29 *Which of you by taking thought can add one cubit unto his stature? (KJV)*

February 11

WHEN THINGS DON'T GO THE WAY YOU WANT THEM TO

When things don't go the way you would like them to, remember, they are going exactly the way they are supposed to! Do not long for the absence of problems in your life. That is an unrealistic goal, since by living in this world you will always have trouble.

Learning to submit to God means learning to trust and follow Him—even when you don't think His way makes sense.

Begin each day anticipating problems and asking Me to help you with whatever difficulty you will encounter. Discuss everything with Me. Remember, I am on your side and I have overcome the world. What more could you want?

John 16:33 *I have told you these things, so that in me you may have peace. In this world you will have trouble. But take heart! I have overcome the world!* (NIV)

◆ February 12 ◆

DRESS LIKE A LADY

A Christian woman must know the proper way to dress. It is more than clothing. Dressing is a language that communicates. A Godly woman should dress in a manner that does not draw attention to her in a physical sense. This is often difficult for many women, for they want to be noticed.

A Godly woman is always concerned with bringing glory to God by virtue of her example and her expression in clothing.

Our dress must reflect the glory of God and not our desire for flattery. We live in a world that fosters seduction and the liberty of vain imagination.

Simply put—don't wear clothing that is seductive and encourages flirtation and lust.

1 Peter 3:2-5 *While they behold your chaste conversation coupled with fear. Whose adorning let it not be that outward adorning of plaiting the lair and of wearing gold or of putting on apparel.* (KJV)

◆ February 13 ◆

MY WAY IS THE RIGHT WAY

Refresh yourself in the peace of my presence. I am not only with you, but I'm within you. I will always go ahead of you to show you the way. I am next to you to hold your hand and I am behind you to pick you up when you fall.

I am your constant companion and your burden-bearer. Remember, I conquered the world, so what more can you want?

I will instill constant peace and joy in you and your companion until the day I call you home.

Do not fear as you walk along the path, not knowing which way to go. If you turn right, you may go off the road. If you turn left, you might fall. Continue walking the path straight ahead to me. My way is the right way.

Revelation 3:20 *Behold, I stand at the door and knock. If any man hear my voice and open the door I will come in to him, and will sup with him and he with me. (KJV)*

February 14

I WILL GIVE YOU PEACE

Thank Me for your problems. As soon as your mind starts to fret, bring it to Me with thanks. You ask, "How can I thank you for the hardship and pain I am going through? If you were a good God you would not allow me to go through this."

I have allowed you to experience this for it brings you closer to Me. As you turn your attention to Me, your problem will subside. As you talk to Me, I will ease the pain. I will lift the problem out of today and cast it into the future.

In its place I will give you peace—the only peace that flows from My presence.

Philippians 4:7-9 *And the peace of God, which passeth all understanding, shall keep your hearts and minds through Christ Jesus. (KJV)*

February 15

GOD'S TIMING IS PERFECT

For the people of Ancient Rome, the festival of Lupercalia was an annual ritual believed to ward off evils spirits and increase fertility. Lupercalia (also known as Februatio, from which comes the month name February) was popular among the new converts to the fast rising Catholic Church.

Valentines Day represents a day of love and friendship. These are wonderful things and God is not opposed to romance at the right time in the right way.

Instead of pagan days and practices, our focus should be on the festivals God has given us in the Bible, which points us to His amazing and incomparable plan for all humanity.

God is always working toward a grand goal, which is the climax of His purpose on earth. He does all things on time according to His schedule, not ours.

Never question His timing. He is perfect and in total control of everything.

John 3:16 *For God so loved the world that he gave his only begotten Son, that whosoever believeth in him should not perish but have everlasting life. (KJV)*

February 16

FORGET YOUR PROBLEMS BY FOCUSING ON OTHERS

When things seem to be going wrong, stop and affirm your trust in Me. Calmly, bring those problems to Me and leave them in my hands. Walk away and remember them no more.

Rejoice in Me and trust in Me. I will make you strong and steady in your walk. You will not stumble or fall, but will walk straight and tall. Take time to rest by the wayside, for I am in no hurry.

Forget your problems by looking to the needs of others. Happiness comes when you shift the focus away from yourself.

You serve Me best through serving others.

Proverbs 24:16 *For the righteous falls seven times and rises again, but the wicked stumble in times of calamity. (NIV)*

February 17

KEEP GOD FIRST

In life you try to please others, only to get hurt and discouraged. Seek to please Me first. Many peoples' decisions are spontaneous and made without thinking them through first. Most of the times this leads to disappointment and heartache.

If you constantly look to other people for answers and validation, pray about this and ask Me to help you stop doing this.

Most people desire only to please themselves or others. This is not my Way for you. When my presence is your deepest delight, you will know immediately what will please me.

Make it your goal to have a deep, intimate relationship with me, seek My pleasure in all you do, and I will never let you down.

***Galatians* 1:10** *For am I now seeking the approval of man or of God? Or am I trying to please man? If I were still trying to please man, I would not be a servant of Christ. (ESV)*

February 18

BE THANKFUL FOR EVERYTHING

A thankful attitude opens doors and windows to My home in Heaven. Spiritual blessings will fall to you from those openings. Moreover, as you look up, you will get a glimpse of your eternal home.

Although it is not yet your time to live here, you will get a vision at how wonderful and beautiful it is. There is no pain, tears, or hatred. There is nothing but love and peace.

Here, there is no one blind, deaf, or crippled. There is only peace, happiness, love, and joy. Your title to Heaven is given freely to you if you accept that I sent My only begotten son to die on the cross for you.

Revelation 21:4 *And God will wipe away every tear from their eyes; there shall be no more death, nor sorrow, nor crying. There shall be no more pain, for the former things have passed away. (KJV)*

February 19

GOD IS REAL

I am closer than you think. You are connected to me by a bond that nobody or nothing can ever sever. If you feel like I'm not there, open your eyes and you will find me.

This is no fantasy or escape. I am real and I am here. I am far more real than the world you live in and the people you see and the things you hear.

Have faith, for it is the confirmation of things you cannot see and the things you cannot hear.

I am far more real than anyone you know. I am the ONLY one you will spend eternal life with. I am not a fairytale in a book. I was, I am, and I always will be.

Matthew 7:13-14 *Enter through the narrow gate. For wide is the gate and broad is the road that leads to destruction and many enter through it. (NIV)*

February 20

AN UNDERSTANDING GOD

Come to Me for understanding. Don't try to figure things out on your own, for you will get discouraged and frustrated. Trying to figure problems and difficult situations on your own is senseless.

I understand everything about you, for I am the one who created you. I know every hair on your head, and when and how you will leave this troubled world and come to live in eternal happiness with Me.

When nobody else understands you, simply draw closer to Me. Rejoice in the one who understands and loves you unconditionally. As I fill you with my love, you will become an example for others to follow.

There is no one who knows you better than I do for I made you. If you seek Me, you will find me.

***Jeremiah* 33:3** *Call to me and I will answer thee, and show thee great and unsearchable things you do not know. (KJV)*

February 21

YOUR GLASS IS HALF FULL

Laughter is the best medicine. It is an amazing gift from God. It helps you cope with sadness of everyday life.

Laughter is really a miracle, for it heals the soul.

Have you ever felt mad or sad and then someone said something to make you laugh? Even though you were still upset, the laughter made your heart better.

It's always good to have a cheerful heart and laugh with family or friends. It is your choice to be sad or happy. Try to find something good in everything. Make your glass always half full, not empty.

Luke 6:21 *Blessed are ye that hunger now: for ye shall be filled. Blessed are ye that weep now: for ye shall laugh. (KJV)*

February 22

YOU ARE MY GREATEST CREATION

Come to Me and listen closely. I am with you wherever you are—nothing can separate you from Me. When I cried out on the cross, "It's finished," the temple was torn in two, from the top to the bottom. This opened the way for you to meet Me face to face.

I am the Creator of the Universe. I made the birds, the ocean, the animals and I made My greatest creation—YOU! I created you in My own image--- giving you dominion over the fish of the sea, the birds of the heavens, and over every creeping thing that creeps on the earth.

Be grateful that I gave you life, no matter what obstacles may arise. The end of the story is a good one. You will return to where you came from and live in eternal peace with ME.

Colossians 1:16 *For by Him all things were created, in heaven and earth, visible and invisible, whether thrones or dominions or rulers or authorities---all things were created through him and for him.* (ESV)

February 23

WORSHIP

Some people worship money, while others idolize other people. Worshiping anybody or anything other than Me is a sin.

Unfortunately, many Christians have a skewed, idealized definition of idols.

An idol is any person, object, or activity that you give a higher priority in your life other than a relationship with Me.

An idol can be your home, a job, a relationship or a pet. An idol can be the work you do that consumes all your energy and time. I am a jealous God and I want all your time and attention.

The Bible says its better to obey than sacrifice. When I say to repent, you must repent. I love you and have a plan for each of you, but only in my parameters.

Chronicles 7:14 *Then if the people who are called by my name will humble themselves and pray and seek my face and turn from their wicked ways, I will hear from heaven and will forgive their sins and heal their land. (KJV)*

February 24

ADULTERY

Many people turn to scripture to find the definition of adultery and how it applies to marriage and divorce.

Adultery refers to the act of a married individual having sexual relations with someone other than their spouse.

57% of American men and 54% of women admit to committing adultery in a relationship.

God's word tells us just how harmful adultery can be, but it also speaks of grace and mercy from a loving God.

Scripture has a lot to say about cheating and its sinful nature. Even if its not cheating on your spouse, cheating has to do with deception and God hates deception.

Stay away from the temptation and schemes of Satan. Adultery is not only a sin against one's mate, but an attack on the sanctity of marriage, and a sin against God.

Prepare yourself with the way God instructs you to see all of His commands are good---not the world's way.

Matthew 5:27-28 *You have heard that it was said, 'You shall not commit adultery'. But I tell you that everyone who looks at a woman with lustful intent has already committed adultery with her in his heart. (KJV)*

February 25

A LIE IS A LIE

I laugh whenever I hear someone say, 'I wasn't lying. It was just a little white lie. It doesn't mean anything.' A lie is a lie—no matter if it's white, black, or purple. Fibs, bluffs, half-truths—they are all lies.

There are six things that I hate--- seven that are an abomination to Me, and three that really break my heart: haughty eyes, a lying tongue, and hands that shed innocent blood.

The Bible is clear to say that lying is a sin and is displeasing to Me--your Father, God. The very first sin in the world involved a lie told to Eve.

Because of that one lie told in the Garden of Eden there is sin in the world and we must all pay the price. Do not lie about anything. A lying tongue is not only something I hate, but it's an abomination to Me.

Psalm 101:7 *No one who practices deceit shall dwelt in my house; no one who utters lies shall continue before my eyes. (ESV)*

February 26

YOU MAY BE LONELY, BUT YOU ARE NEVER ALONE

No one likes to be alone. Sometimes as Christians we will have to be alone. At these times we are to build a stronger relationship with the Lord by drawing closer to Him in prayer. If we kept our focus on the Lord we would know and understand that we are NEVER alone. God is always close by, and guess what--- He is near right now.

You may feel lonely at times, but remember you are never alone.

Ask God to give you comfort. Talk to Him like you would your best friend for He won't turn away from you. He never shuts you out or criticizes you. He is the ultimate comforter and friend.

Philippians 4:6 *Do not be anxious about anything, but in everything by prayer and supplication with thanksgiving let your requests be made known to God. (NKJV)*

February 27

L-O-V-E

The word "love" has many different meanings. It can have affectionate, strong liking, romantic, or sexual implications. Love is one of the attributes of God and an essential part of His nature. Our relationship to God is like the loving relationship between a child and parent.

God knows and deeply cares for each of us. He is our Father, and like a good father, at times He might have to submit tough love on us.

Jesus said that our most important responsibility in life is to love God. How do we do that? We do that by obeying his commandments and putting our trust in Him by prayer and maintaining a humble attitude.

Loving God with all your heart is easy: Aim to make Him your greatest treasure in life--- nothing else comes close.

Mark 12:31 *The second (Commandment) is this, 'You shall love your neighbor as yourself.' There is no other commandment greater than these. (ESV)*

February 28

LIVING IN THE END TIMES

We are living in the times that the Bible speaks of as, "The last days." Many people are afraid to die and of the unknown. Because we are in the end times, we know according to the prophecy it will be a time of tribulation and trouble.

That is enough to frighten anyone. There is only one way we can ease the fear in a world of turmoil--- It is only through God's power that we can walk in peace and safety.

We must give ourselves totally up to the Lord and yield to His will as to what He wants us to do. This means a total commitment and putting God first—before time, money, family and careers.

As we listen to the Holy Spirit, He speaks something positive for us to do. By obeying Him, praying and reading the Bible, we can get free from bondage by submitting to God.

Psalm 112:7 *He shall not be afraid of evil tidings; his heart is fixed, trusting in the Lord.* (KJV)

FOR MARRIAGE COUPLES ONLY

God gives us very clear guidance in His word on how we can best experience the gift of intimacy and love. Sex was meant as a wonderful experience between a husband and a wife to provide physical, emotional, and spiritual bonding. Sex is not bad in God's eyes-- in a Godly perspective--- sex is a good thing.

He created humans, "male and female" and viewed what He had made as being "very good." God reserves sexual relations for married couples only.

The Bible promotes complete abstinence before marriage. Sex between husband and wife is the only form of sexual relations of which God approves.

If the message on sex before marriage were obeyed, there would be far less abortions, pregnancies, and diseases. Abstinence saves lives, and most important honors God.

Galatians 5:19 *The acts of the flesh are obvious: sexual immorality, impurity and debauchery; idolatry and witchcraft; hatred, discord, jealousy, fits of rage and the like. (NIV)*

MARCH

March 1

AVOID TEMPTATIONS

Temptations are inevitable. Yet, many Christians yield to temptations. Sometimes they are subtle, and sometimes they are more obvious.

Though we are not free from temptations, we are free of the bondage it breeds. The devil will often use fiery darts that consume our mind. These fiery darts come in the form of a lie, a thought of rejection, wrong doctrine, or a deprecating thought.

The classic symptom that a Believer has yielded to temptation is discouragement. Christians who are perpetually discouraged are the most difficult to influence for the glory of God and the furtherance of the gospel of Jesus Christ.

This is why Jesus said, "*Watch and pray that ye enter not into temptation: the spirit indeed is willing, but the flesh is weak.*" Matthew 26:4 1a *KJV.*

The key to overcoming temptation is the reality and reliability of God's word. The Holy Spirit will never direct us contrary to the Word of God.

Matthew 26: 41 *Watch and pray that you may not enter into temptation. The spirit indeed is willing, but the flesh is weak. (KJV)*

March 2

PATIENCE IS A VIRTUE

Patience is a virtue. Many of us have a hard time learning to wait on things. We want them NOW and don't want to wait for them.

Trusting in God is the first step in learning to be patient. Why fret and worry? It does no good. You know God loves you and will do what's best for you, so the next time you feel like you are losing it, pray for God's guidance or intervention.

You are God's partner, and like a partner in a business, you must be patient, loyal, and work together.

Thank Him for trusting in you to be His partner.

James 2:26 *As the body without the spirit is dead, so faith without deeds is dead.* (NIV)

March 3

IT'S YOUR BIRTHDAY

It's that time of year again. It's your birthday! When you were young you couldn't wait until you would be sixteen so you could drive a car. Then you wanted to be eighteen so you could legally drink alcohol. (Average age in most states)

Twenty-one was that magical number that meant you're an adult. Forty is a number that most of us feel is the turning point and after reaching this many begin to count backwards for we see our life is flying by.

When the first number in your age changes, do you panic, get depressed and evaluate where you are and have been in life?

Do not sit back in a rocking chair waiting for your number to be up.

Live life each day, as it was your last. I am preparing your place in Heaven for when it is your time-- until that day comes, enjoy your life in serving me, and others. Life isn't over yet!

James 4:14 *Why, you do not even know what will happen tomorrow. What is your life? You are a mist that appears for a little while and then vanishes. (NIV)*

March 4

I WILL NEVER LEAVE OR FORSAKE YOU

Nothing can separate you from my love. Whenever you feel anxious or scared, remember this. Keep repeating the phrase:

I will never leave you or forsake you.

At times you will endure trials so difficult you wonder how you'll get through it. But as Christians you were designed by me to endure and spiritually prosper from life's trials.

Being human, whenever I am overtook by fear, I say this psalm and it always calms me. "*The Lord is my shepherd; I shall not want. He makes me lie down in green pastures. He leads me beside still waters. He restores my soul. He leads me in paths of righteousness for his names sake. Even though I walk through the valley of the shadow of death, I will fear no evil, for you are with me; your rod and staff, they comfort me. You prepare a table before me in the presence of my enemies; you anoint my head with oil' my cup overflows". (ESV)*

When you feel scared, repeat the saying above and I assure it will comfort you.

Deuteronomy 31:8 *It is the Lord who goes before you. He will be with you; he will not leave you or forsake you. Do not fear or be dismayed. (NIV)*

March 5

SEARCHING FOR LOVE IN ALL THE WRONG PLACES

Many people spend a lifetime searching for someone who understands them. They go through dozens of relationships, looking for that special someone. Hearts will be broken, and time after time you will discover that there is not one person who will ever fill all your dreams or know the intimacies of your heart, mind, and soul.

God is the only one who knows everything about you and He loves you despite any faults you may have. Your relationship with God is vital to your Christian walk; but your dating life, the health of your marriage, and your family relationships also reflect on your personal walk with the Lord.

If you are single, don't look for that special someone. When it is the right time God will send him/her to you.

Corinthians 13:13 *So now faith, hope and love abide, these three; but the greatest of these is love. (ESV)*

March 6

THE GREEN-EYED MONSTER

Jealousy is also known as the green-eyed monster. We all have met him once or twice. Some of you may be familiar with him for he could be living inside you right now.

When we fall into the pit of jealousy, we spiral downward very quickly.

Jealousy is such a powerful force that we often need God's words to help us overcome it.

You can be jealous of someone's beauty or what they have, but being jealous indicates that we are not satisfied with what God has given us. In order to overcome jealousy we need to become more like Jesus and less like ourselves.

Jealousy is insecurity--- that you are lacking self-worth. But know that YOU ARE worthy, for you are a child of the highest.

Proverbs 6:34 *For jealousy makes a man furious and he will not spare when he takes revenge. (ESV)*

March 7

SOUL SLEEP

Sleep is a mandatory part of your life. It refreshes you to wake up and start all over again. But what does God say about, "Soul sleep?" Is it Biblical or Heretical?

Soul sleep is the belief that the souls of the dead are unconscious until the Second Coming of Christ. When the Bible speaks of a saint as being "asleep" it is speaking of their body---not their soul.

In the Old Testament the saints were not in an unconscious state while in the "paradise" section of the underworld. When a Christian dies (before the rapture) they are immediately in the presence of Christ. Death has lost its sting.

When Christ returns, our bodies will rise incorruptible. The grace and death are dead. Biblically speaking, soul sleep is heresy.

Revelation 6:10 *The souls of some martyrs cry out and ask God, "How long, O Lord, holy and true, dost thou not judge and avenge our blood on them that dwell on the earth? (KJV)*

March 8

A THIN LINE BETWEEN LOVE AND HATE

There is a thin line between love and hate. Both are very intense emotions, but at opposite ends of the pendulum. Love flows from the heart, whereas hate needs to be fed so it can grow.

Feeding hate takes time, energy, and steals all joy away from you.

Who are you hurting? Not the person you have ill feelings towards, but yourself.

When you feel hate for a person, pray for them and ask God to take the hatred away.

Biblically speaking, there are positive and negative aspects to hatred. Hatred is a poison that destroys us from within, producing bitterness that eats away at our hearts and minds. Hatred also destroys the personal witness of a Christian because it removes him from fellowship with the Lord.

It is just as easy to love, as it is to hate: So when you have negative feelings or bitterness, pray to God to take it away and replace it with His love.

Proverbs 10:12 *Hatred stirs up strife, but love covers all offenses. (KJV)*

March 9

GOD IS STILL WRITING YOUR STORY

I got a message today from our Father. He told me that you are troubled and worried about something. He is sad that you don't have enough trust in Him to know that He is in control and everything will be okay.

Whether it is a financial situation, a relationship, or health problem---everything is going to work out for the good. You see: **He is not done writing your story**. Although you don't know what the outcome will be, he wants you to know that it will be okay.

Each one of us has our own unique story, and God is the author of every one. They are all different, but are all best sellers! So, don't fret because He is not done writing yours yet!

2 Peter 2:9 *Then the Lord knows how to rescue the Godly from trials, and to keep the unrighteousness under punishment until the day of judgment. (ESV)*

March 10

APPRECIATE ALL THINGS

Learn to appreciate everything. Be stimulated by the afflictions you encounter along your journey. Together, we can move mountains.

Look back and see how I removed you from one of the most difficult times in your life. At the time you thought you wouldn't make it, but in the end you prevailed.

Life will throw you good times and it will throw bad times. There will be times when you aren't sure which way to go.

Fear not---I am there by your side, holding your right hand.

We will make it as we always have, and always will.

John16:33 *I have said these things to you, that in me you may have peace. In the world you will have tribulation. But take heart: I have overcome the world. (ESV)*

March 11

WHEN ONE DOOR CLOSES, I WILL OPEN ANOTHER

As you get older, it may seem you have lost your value, for it may be harder to find a job. Although you have a lot to offer an employer, many would rather hire someone younger, prettier, or for less money.

Don't lose faith. Have patience, for I am in control. You may not get that job you want because I know it is not the right job for you, but I have something better for you!

Ask me to give you patience, faith, and hope. When one door closes another will open. I am the one who is holding the doorknob.

Psalm 25:8 *Good and upright is the Lord; therefore will he teach sinners in the way. (KJV)*

March 12

LOSING A LOVED ONE

You have just said goodbye to someone you love. You're tired and emotionally spent. You're afraid to take the next step without him/her by your side.

Take a deep breath and pray. Call a friend and tell them how you feel and then talk to me. I know your grief and the pain you are feeling.

I will get you through this. It is hard to start all over again once you have been with someone a long time. It is scary and overwhelming, but it doesn't have to be.

Remember, I too, was alone once. I left my mother and my twelve best friends. I walked toward Golgatha, bearing the heavy weight of the cross that carried all your sins.

But I was never alone. My Father, God, was there, as He is with you.

Matthew 8:5 *And when Jesus had entered into Capernaum, there came unto him a centurion, beseeching him. (KJV)*

March 13

CONTROL YOUR TEMPER

My mother used to cook with a pressure cooker. The purpose was that water would boil by building up pressure inside a closed pot. This way the food would cook quicker. She was careful to make sure the lid was sealed tight, for if it weren't, the lid could blow off, hurting whoever was close by.

The same can be said about someone who has a bad temper. Whenever they are upset, they can explode. Some people can hold their temper better than others. I learned to count to 10 before losing mine. It's something that needs practicing and doesn't happen overnight.

Counting to 10 gives you a chance to cool down and not say anything you will be sorry for later. Once those words come out you cannot take them back. We should be careful of what our tongue speaks, for the uncontrolled tongue is especially harmful and dangerous to others and the body of Christ.

Proverbs 21:23 *Whoever keeps his mouth and his tongue keeps himself out of trouble. (ESV)*

March 14

JESUS CAN CURE ALL

In the days of ancient times there were many diseases that we do not see today. One was leprosy. It was an infectious disease that caused severe disfiguring skin sores and nerve damage. People who had leprosy were ostracized and shunned as outcasts.

Jesus cured many people of this disease. They were known as "unclean" and would wear torn clothes to cover the lower part of their faces.

Naaman was one of those who Jesus healed. Others who were said to have this disease at one time were Moses, Miriam, Gehazi, Joab, Uzziah and Simon.

Todays' diseases are Aids, Malaria, Cholera, Cancer and Heart Disease. If you or a loved one is fighting a disease, know that with God nothing is impossible. He can cure ***anything***.

Psalm 103: 2-4 *Bless the Lord, O my soul, and forget not all his benefits, who forgives all your iniquity, who heals all your disease, who redeems your life from the pit, who crowns you with steadfast love and mercy. (ESV)*

March 15

THERE ARE NO MISTAKES IN LIFE

We all experience times when we don't know which way to go. We are confused in which direction to take. We are afraid if we choose the wrong way, we cannot go back and start over.

Of course you don't want to make a mistake, but they really are not mistakes. They are lessons you must learn from, so you don't do the same thing over again and again.

The world is a big school, life is a learning place, and we are all students. God gives each and every one of us a different lesson. Although they may seem harsh at the time, He is our Father and just like our earthly Father, He loves us and wants the best for us.

The next time you are unsure of something that arises in your life, wait before you react. Pray to God for his discernment and wait for his answer. He will never steer you wrong!

Psalm 37:24 *Though he fall, he shall not be cast headlong, for the Lord upholds his hand.* (ESV)

March 16

THE RIGHT KIND OF WEALTH

There is no promise in the Bible that says being a Christian will lead to a good job, wealth, and freedom from debt. In Jesus' time it was a common belief that great wealth was a sign of God's favor, and poverty was God's punishment for sin.

Jesus denied this thought. Despite the Bible's warnings against it, the idea that wealth is a sign of God's favor and that the poor have done something wrong to deserve their condition is totally wrong.

Those of us who are blessed with wealth beyond our needs have a responsibility to share generously with those who are less fortunate. The craving of wealth and possessions can lead you into all kinds of temptations. Do not wear yourself out to get rich--- have the wisdom to show restraint.

True, everlasting beauty, and wealth, are found within.

1 Timothy 6:10 *For the love of money is a root of all kinds of evil. Some people, eager for money have wandered from the faith and pierced themselves with many gifts. (KJV)*

March 17

ABSTINENCE

Is sex before marriage considered sexually immoral? The answer according to 1 Corinthians 7:2 is "yes." But in todays world there is so much immorality that each man should have his own wife and each woman should have her own husband.

Sex within marriage is pleasurable, and God designed it that way. He wants men and women to enjoy sexual activity within the confines of marriage.

Abstinence is God's only policy when it comes to sex before marriage. It saves lives, protects babies, gives sexual relations the proper value, and honors God.

You must follow a different philosophy based on Christian truth and Scripture. The key to this philosophy is relationship. Sex before marriage can result in so many wrong choices and is a great instability in the relationship.

If your partner is determined to have sex before marriage, and won't take 'no' for an answer, perhaps its time to move on.

Corinthians 6:18 *Flee from sexual immorality. All other sins a person commits are outside the body, but whoever sins sexually, sins against their own body. (KJV)*

March 18

DREAMS DO COME TRUE

You have a dream. Dreams can be wonderful. They are visions of what you want or want to do. The Bible defines a dream in Job 33:15, *"In a dream, in a vision of the night, when deep sleep falleth upon men, in slumberings upon the bed."* (KJV)

But many times people don't have patience waiting for their dream to come to fruition. They lose their focus on the goal they believe God has given them.

Keep pressing on-- even when it gets tough, don't be discouraged! Remember, dreams are thoughts God puts in our minds that we are capable of reaching. Enjoy this partnership in accomplishing His work.

God can do anything. If they are His will, your dreams will come true! It may not happen when you want it to, but it will in God's timing.

Ecclesiastes 5:7 *For in the multitude of dreams and many words there are also (divers) vanities; but fear thou God.* (KJV)

March 19

DEALING WITH ANXIETY

In todays world there is so much hatred, worry, and uncertainty. How do you deal with it? Many have sought counsel from the word of God when faced with worry and anxiety, and for a good reason. This is much better than trying to find comfort from a bottle of a bottle of pills.

Life can be overwhelming at times--- especially in today's ever-increasing complexity. We worry about finances, our families, job interviews, and endless taxes.

Anxiety in your heart wears you down and makes you physically and mentally sick. When you find yourself worrying, take out your Bible and read one of the many verses it teaches you about worry and anxiety. *(Matthew 6:34 NIV Therefore, do not worry about tomorrow, for tomorrow will worry about itself.)*

Saying and believing in this will calm you and give you peace.

Matthew 11:28-30 *Come to me all you who are weary and burdened and I will give you rest. Take my yoke upon you and learn from me, for I am gentle and humble in heart, and you will find rest for your souls. For my yoke is easy and my burden is light. (NIV)*

◆ March 20 ◆

GREED---NEVER HAVING ENOUGH

Greed is a strong and selfish desire to have more of something; most often, money or power. Greed can destroy a friendship, relationship, or tear a family apart. This usually occurs over money or material things. You see this especially when someone dies. People turn ugly. The vultures are loose and the claws come out!

Greed and a desire for riches are traps that bring ruin and destruction. It is the love of money and not money itself that is the problem.

Greed refuses to be satisfied. More often than not, the more we get, the more we want. Material possessions will not protect us in this life or eternally.

"Be on your guard against all kinds of greed: a man's life does not consist in the abundance of his possessions." Luke 12:15 KJV

When we become greedy and not happy with what we have, we are not giving God the glory and worship He deserves.

Hebrews 13:5 *Keep your life free from money, and be content with what you have, for he has said, "I will never leave you nor forsake you."* (NIV)

March 21

GOD'S PEACE

Thank Me for your problems. You are quick to thank Me for your blessings, but when you have a problem, you fret, curse, and become depressed.

When your mind starts thinking about negative difficulties that arise in your life, ask Me how to handle the problem. Thank me for the situation with thanksgiving.

Most of todays concerns are usually leftovers from the past that still haunt you. If you give it to me, I will take it and deposit it into the future. The problem will fade and lose all the power it has on you.

Life is bound to bring you problems and heartaches for the world you live in is a broken, fallen one. The only peace you will get is by giving the problem to Me. In return, I will give you MY peace, which flows freely from Me.

John 16:33 *I have told you these things to you, that in me you may have peace. In this world you will have trouble. But take heart; I have overcome the world.* (NIV)

March 22

MEN!

Men! Women can't live with them and we can't live without them!

God first created man, and then He created woman by removing a rib from man.

He created woman so man did not have to be alone and so they could have children. So, if God did this, it must be perfect and for the good, because everything He does is right.

Then why is it so hard for these two creatures to live in peace and harmony? If we were meant to be biological partners, shouldn't it be easy to work as a team?

A woman's power is the direct opposite of a man's. When two opposing powers join into one force, an entirely new force emerges-- one that has much more intensity than either one individually. Since the beginning of time, man and woman have had a love/hate relationship. But God wants His two most precious creations to love one another and live in peace.

Next time your partner upsets you, take a minute to pray. By the time you are done, most likely you will forget what you were mad about.

Genesis 2:18 *Then the Lord God said, "It is not good that the man should be alone. I will make him a helper fit for him." (ESV)*

March 23

SISTERS

It's a natural thing to love your sister, just like it's natural to love yourself. Scripture teaches us to love other Christians like you love your siblings.

If you have a sister, cherish her. Thank the Lord for your sister, who is also your best friend.

Continually pray for your sister and love her. Family is a wonderful gift from God and sisters have a unique bond that lasts for a lifetime.

The Bible starts talking about siblings in Genesis and mentions brothers and sisters many times after that. Jesus had brothers and sisters and preaches that we are to love and be kind to them.

Jesus said, "*A new commandment I give to you, that you love one another, just as I have loved you, you also are to love one another.*" *John 13:34 (NIV)*

Call your sister today and tell her how much she means to you, whether it's a blood sister or a sister in Christ.

James 4:11 *Brothers and sisters, do not slander one another. Anyone who speaks against a brother or sister or judges them speaks against the law, you are not keeping it, but sitting in judgment on it. (NIV)*

March 24

WALKING WITH JESUS

Seek My face. You are just beginning your journey with Me. It is not an easy road, for there will be a lot of turns and bumps along the way. Don't fear, for I will be there with you the entire way. When you feel like you are going to fall, I will hold you up. When you don't know which way to go, I will lead you down the right path. Trust Me, for I am your rock and strength.

I have said these things to you: "That in me you may have peace. In the world you will have tribulation, but take heart for I have overcome the world."

My father, God, puts bumps in the road in your journey called life, but remember: He does this to strengthen your faith in Him. Do not disappoint Him or Me. As My child, do as I do and you will live a life filled with peace, love and contentment.

John 16:33 *I have told you these things so that in Me you may have peace. You will have suffering in this world. Be courageous! I have conquered the world!* (CSB)

March 25

WHAT IS A CHRISTIAN?

A Christian can be defined as a person who has by faith received and fully trusted in Jesus Christ as the only Savior from sin.

There are a lot of fake Christians—people professing to be a Christian, but are really not. Yet, they complacently remain convinced that all is well with their soul and relationship with Jesus.

The clear teaching of the Bible is that when someone is saved, his life will most definitely change, as he is a "new creation."

Examine yourself to see if you are in faith. Have you been re-created?

Luke 6:46 *And why call ye me, Lord, Lord, and do not the things which I say? (KJV)*

March 26

A MIGHTY GOD

I am a mighty God. Nothing is too difficult for Me. When you face unexpected situations, there is no reason to panic. What I require from you is only to stay connected to me.

Talk with me. Listen to what I have to say. I am not a God that will leave His children alone and troubled. When I allow difficulties in your life, I already know how and when it will end.

Trust in me. Faith is all I ask of you. It is the most important thing in a Christian's life. You cannot buy it, sell it, or give it away. It is the greatest gift you can give me.

Faith is a "means to a new beginning."

Hebrew 11:1 *Now faith is the substance of things hoped for, the evidence of things not seen. (KJV)*

March 27

STOP WORRYING!

Stop all your worrying! Your busy mind shuttles back and forth, weaving a web of confusion and doubt. If you open the Bible you can read scripture that will help you deal with uncertainty in life.

Life can be overwhelming at times, especially in today's complex and broken world. You have to learn how to alleviate yourself from worry and anxiety by meditating on My word and casting your cares and worries on Me. I am your ultimate source of peace, hope, strength, courage and joy.

According to the Bible there is nothing wrong with realistically acknowledging and trying to deal with the identifiable problems of life. Such worry must be committed to prayer to Me, your Heavenly Father--- the only one who can release you from paralyzing fear or anxiety.

Colossians 3:15 *Let the peace of Christ rule in your hearts, since as members of one body you were called to peace. And be thankful. (NIV)*

March 28

SICKNESS COMES FROM SATAN

Why does God allow sickness and disease? The key is remembering that God's ways are higher than our ways. When you are suffering with a sickness or disease you should focus on what good God might bring as a result.

Many times people who were once sick remember that through it all God never left them, and in the end it brought them closer to Him, they learned to trust Him more, and learned how precious and valuable life is.

Remember, some forms of sickness doesn't come from God, but from Satan. But even during those trying times-- God is in control. He sometimes allows sickness for His perfect will and purpose.

God is good, even when you are suffering.

Romans 5:3-4 *More than that, we rejoice in our sufferings, knowing that suffering produces endurance and endurance produces character and character produces hope. (ESV)*

March 29

LOVE IS A WONDERFUL THING

Love is such a wonderful thing. It is not only an emotion, but it's an act of the will and commitment.

There are many songs and books written about love. The first and most important thing we must recognize about love is that it is all about God. Love originated from the Trinity: The Father, the Son and Holy Spirit.

Without the Father loving the Son and the Spirit, without the Son loving the Father and the Spirit, and without the Spirit loving the Father and the Son, we would know nothing of love because it would not exist.

Just as God's love for us in Christ was sacrificial, so should our love be for each other.

John 3:16 *For God so loved the world, that He gave His only Son, that whoever believes in Him should not perish but have eternal life. (ESV)*

March 30

AN UNCOORDINATED PERSON

Many of us are uncoordinated. I could not walk a straight line if my life depended on it. Slipping not only on the street, but in my faith.

But God's love always was there to support me and pick me up. When I slip in my faith, He is there to steady me. This act of His unconditional love made me realize God's supportive love that is visible to my slippery-soul. His love is much more powerful than I know.

Psalm 94: 18 *When I said, "My foot is slipping" your unfailing love, Lord, supported me.* (NIV)

March 31

DOGS: GOD SPELLED BACKWARD

They say dog is a man's best friend. In fact, did you realize that dog spelled backward is God? In the beginning God created the earth and all the creatures on it to be under the authority of humanity.

Because of man's sinful nature, some people abuse animals sometimes without realizing it. Abuse of anything that God made is not the character of God, but rather of the Evil One.

God's intention was to bless mankind with a wonderful world of creatures that we could love and enjoy, but He also holds us responsible as to how we treat them.

Animals have always had a significant role throughout different parts of Scripture. Treat animals with the love and respect, as God wants you to.

Ecclesiastes 3:19 *Humans and animals have the same destiny. One dies just like the other. All of them have the same breath of life, and man has no advantage over the beasts, for all is vanity.* (GW)

APRIL

April 1

GETTING THROUGH TOUGH TIMES

Remember, having joy in your life does not depend on your circumstances. People who are wealthy and seem to have everything many times are the unhappiest. They strive to get to the top of the ladder, only to discover that when they reach it, they are alone.

You will have difficulties in life, so do not let these temporary setbacks get you down and pull you away from Me. Instead, look to Me and I will get you through even the toughest times.

Apostle Paul was joyful at all times: through the good and the bad.

Many of these problems will eventually resolve themselves, but knowing I am there to help you get through the tough times will make it tolerable, so you can find peace, even in the most difficult days.

1 Timothy 6:17-19 *As for the rich in this present age, charge them not be haughty, nor to set their hopes on the uncertainty of riches, but on God, who richly provides us with everything to enjoy. (ESV)*

April 2

GOD IS IN CONTROL

There are many times when you will feel like you can't take it anymore. Whether it's related to a family, your spouse, financial, or health problem; you may think of ending it all. Get that thought out of your mind, now!

All things that happen to you are *supposed* to happen --- for a reason! I am the only one who knows what the reason is, and I know how and when this situation will end. Do you think I would let any harm come to one of my children? NO!

I am in control and promise I will help you get through this. One day you will look back and understand why you had to go through it and the pain will subside and fade away. I will take it from you and throw it into the air---- never to return. Thank Me for watching over you and how much I love you.

Ecclesiastes 7:17 *Be not overly wicked, neither be a fool. Why should you die before your time? (ESV)*

April 3

LOVE YOUR NEIGHBOR AS YOU LOVE YOURSELF

The Bible commands us to love God and to love our neighbor as we love ourselves. To be a human is to be in a state of tension between your appetites, your dreams, the social realities around you, and your obligations.

Love is the element--- the most essential one, indeed, that makes the world go round. Without it we are lost as human beings. God has been so gracious, caring, and kind to fill our hearts with love.

Read the Bible sayings and quotes that ensure us that God is Love and we have been created with Love; thus Love is the powerful voice that God uses to speak to us—his loving children.

Ephesians 5:2 *And walk in love, just as Christ also loved you and gave Himself up for us as an offering and a sacrifice to God as a fragrant aroma. (ESV)*

April 4

SEPARATION BY DEATH

The subject of death is very often an unpleasant topic. Most people would just as soon never have to think about it. There are many different ideas on just what death is. There have been several movies offering scenarios of what death and dying might be like.

The Bible presents death as separation. Physical death is the separation of the soul from the body and spiritual death is the separation of the soul from God.

Death is the result of sin. On the cross Jesus experienced physical death.

The difference is that Adam died because he was a sinner and Jesus who never sinned chose to die as a substitute for sinners. For the unsaved, death brings to an end the chance to accept God's gracious offer of salvation. For the saved, death ushers us into the presence of Christ.

John 11:25 *Jesus said to her, "I am the resurrection and the life. Whoever believes in me, though he die, yet shall he live."* (ESV)

April 5

FINDING TRUE HAPPINESS

How can you find happiness in life? We all want to be happy, but sometimes trying to find happiness can be a struggle. Often times we search for it in all the wrong places, people, or things.

Many people ask this question, longing for the answer. They believe that money, fame, or beauty will make them happy. Hence, they pursue such things, only to find that happiness eludes them.

Jesus identified the key to happiness when he said, "Happy are those conscious of their spiritual need."

True happiness can only be found if we take steps to fill our greatest need---our hunger for spiritual truth about God and His purpose for us. Knowing the truth can help us to discern what is really important and what is not.

Proverbs 3:13-18 *Blessed is the one who finds wisdom and the one who gets understanding for the gain from her is better than gain from silver and her profit better than gold. She is more precious than jewels and nothing you desire can compare with her. (ESV)*

April 6

THANK GOD FOR YOUR TALENTS

Why do you feel unworthy and not important? Some people feel they are not as important, smart, or pretty as others!

Then there are those who feel they are so much better than others!

Jesus, Himself, is the best example of humility for He was the only Son of God, yet He was gentle and humble and strong.

Some think being humble means groveling in front of others or believing they are no good and others are better.

But God says when you are humble you are free from pride and arrogance. You know that in your flesh you are inadequate, yet you also know who you are in Christ.

Humility also is recognizing that you need God's help and knowing you can't truly succeed in your own strength. It is thanking God for your talents and gifts and giving Him credit for your accomplishments.

Ephesians 4:31-32 *Get rid of bitterness, rage, anger, brawling and slander, along with every form of malice. Be kind and compassionate to one another, forgiving each other, just as Christ God forgave you. (NIV)*

April 7

DEALING WITH DIFFICULT PEOPLE

We all have had to deal with difficult people at one time in our life. Whether it is a spouse, child, parent, or friend. We find that person impossible to deal with in one way or another.

A difficult person may be one who is condescending, argumentative, belligerent, selfish, obtuse, or simply rude. Difficult people know how, "to push the wrong buttons" and stir up chaos and trouble. Dealing with difficult people becomes an exercise in patience, love, and grace.

In dealing with difficult people we must guard against pride. It is crucial to recall the admonition given by the apostle Paul in Romans 12:3: *"For by the grace given me I say to every one of you: Do not think of yourself more highly than you ought, but rather think of yourself with sober judgment in accordance with the measure of faith God has given you." (NIV)*

By the grace of God we can deal with difficult people through patience, kindness, goodness, faith, gentleness and self-control.

Proverbs 10:12 *Hatred stirs up conflict, but love covers all wrongs. (NIV)*

April 8

HOMOSEXUALITY

Some people think being homosexual is as much outside one's control as the color of your skin and your height. On the other hand, the Bible clearly and consistently declares that homosexual activity is a sin.

This leads to much controversy, debate, and hostility between people. A person may be born with a greater susceptibility to homosexuality, just as some people are born with a tendency to violence and other sins. The problem with homosexual attraction is that it is an attraction to something God has forbidden. As a sinful human being living in a sinful world, we are beset with weaknesses, temptations, and inducements to sin.

Homosexuality is not a greater sin than any other for all sin is offensive to God. Yet, we should not treat homosexuals as if they were lepers for we are to love one another as God loves each and every one of us. And we are not to judge others, for only God can judge.

Corinthians 6:11 *That is what some of you were. But you were washed, you were sanctified, you were justified in the name of the Lord Jesus Christ and by the Spirit of our God. (NIV)*

(Note: Before some of the Corinthians were saved, they lived homosexual lives, but no sin is too great for the cleansing power of Jesus).

April 9

LIVING IN FEAR

Living in todays' world we are living in a time of fear: Fear of violence, fear of man's inhumanity to man, fear of want and fear of war.

The media encourages fear in people through its increased interest in the black arts. Bookstores have entire sections devoted to materials on this subject. There are specialty shops that deal with paraphernalia on witchcraft and the unknown.

When you are controlled by your fears you are in fact making fear a more powerful force in your life than God. Fear can actually hold you back from achieving the goals you have set for yourself in life.

So whenever you feel enveloped in a thick cloud of fear, remember these words: "*When I am afraid, I will trust you. In God, whose word I praise, In God I trust; I will not be afraid. What can mortal man do to me?*" (Psalm 56:3-4) *NIV*

Luke 12:32 *Do not be afraid, little flock, for your Father has been pleased to give you the kingdom. (NIV)*

April 10

A STRONG, INDEPENDENT WOMAN

We all look up to strong, independent women. But how do we become one ourselves?

As Helen Keller quoted, "When we do the best we can, we never know what miracle is wrought in our life, or in the life of another."

If you want to be an independent woman, remember whatever you do, make sure you are different. If you are different, you will stand out in the crowd.

1 Peter 2:16 *As free, and not using your liberty for a cloke of maliciousness, but as the servants of God. (NIV)*

April 11

GIVE THANKS FOR EVERYTHING

Thankfulness is the way to open the door to my presence. I have placed a door between you and me and have empowered you to be the only one to open it.

When you thank me for everything---the good and the bad in your life, the door will begin to open. Being thankful is the foundation—the mortar that builds your house. No storm can destroy it.

When thankfulness comes out of your mouth, the door opens wide, letting the light and warmth in. I want you to learn to give thanks 'in all circumstances.' See how many times you can thank me daily.

One day soon you will be with me and there will be no more worries, tears, or pain.

Revelation 21:4 *And God shall wipe all tears from their eyes, and there will be no more death, neither sorrow, nor crying nor pain. These things of the past are gone forever. (KJV)*

April 12

COME TO ME

When you are weak and weary---come to me. You can rest comfortably and securely in My arms. Do not be ashamed of your weakness. It draws Me closer to you, for I am your Father and want to help you.

Signs of weakness is merely a human trait that I, and I alone, can conquer, for I am strong and omnipotent.

You look around and see others who seem to be carefree and go through life with ease. Do not be envious. They also went through rough journeys, but with My help they came out in victory.

Life can be full of challenges and no matter what you face, be assured that I, your God, am always with you. I know the right direction that will lead you out of the dark.

Matthew 11:28-30 *Come to me, all you who are weary and burdened and I will give you rest. Take my yoke upon you and learn from me, for I am gentle and humble in heart, and you will find rest for your souls. For my yoke is easy and my burden is light. (ESV)*

April 13

LIFE IS FLEETING FAST

When things don't go your way, don't complain--- accept the situation. If you indulge in feelings of regret, they will spill over into resentment.

Don't let the world shatter your thinking and draw you away from Me. It is a challenge to stay focused on Me, and what I have prepared for you. Don't let these insignificant things take the joy out of your life.

Remember, this life is fleeting fast. You will soon be called home to live your eternal life in perfect peace. Why let these small things that occur in your life, steal your happiness?

Do not let anything steal your joy.

John 16:33 *I have said these things to you, that in me you may have peace. In the world you will have trouble. But take heart; I have overcome the world. (NIV)*

April 14

FRIENDS

Friends are a gift from me and must be treated as such. It is hard to find a true friend, and if you are blessed to have one, cherish them.

But remember, I am your best friend. I will always walk hand in hand with you through life. The friendship I offer is unconditional and eternal love. I will never hurt you or abandon you in rough times. I will never cheat on you, steal from you, or lie to you. I am a friend who never judges or puts you down.

There is none like me. The friendship I offer you is practical and down-to-earth, yet it is saturated.

Proverbs 22:24-25 *Make no friendship with a man given to anger, nor go with a wrathful man, lest you learn his ways and entangle yourself in a snare. (ESV)*

April 15

HAVING A GOD MOMENT

We all need a "God Moment." Women multi-task trying to do several things at the same time, but eventually overload and crash.

There is a deep tension that must be balanced when she has to raise a family, tend to the house, and perhaps go to a job to help with the bills.

You get it from all ends: The spouse, the kids, the boss and your parents. That is when you need to take time out for a "God Moment."

Go somewhere quiet. Shut the phone off and close your eyes. Talk to God and ask Him to help get you through the day. Partner with Him for He will never let you down.

So the next time you feel like you can't take it anymore, STOP, go somewhere quiet, and hear the whispers from God. He will calm and assure you.

Philippians 4:6 *Do not be anxious about anything, but in everything by prayer and supplication with thanksgiving let your requests be made known to God. (ESV)*

April 16

SPREAD YOUR WINGS AND FLY

Do you consider yourself to be a strong person? Being strong does not mean you have to be muscular and bulky on the outside--- it means being strong on the inside.

Strong enough to stand up for what you believe is right. Not caving in to what someone else believes just because you want him to like you.

Unfortunately, many people choose to live inside the box. There they feel safe, for there are no rules. They will not be judged or criticized. But God doesn't want you to live in the box.

He wants you to be strong and willing to bend and to be who you really are. He made you unique and an individual, and there is nobody like you. Remember, God makes no mistakes, so be the person you were born to be. Climb outside the box, spread your wings and fly.

2 *Timothy* 2:15 *Do your best to present yourself to God as one approved, a worker who has no need to be ashamed, rightly handling the word of truth. (ESV)*

April 17

VANITY

What is vanity? Vanity is having an excessive pride in one's looks, appearance, status, or abilities, compared to that of others.

It is someone who has the quality of being conceited, narcissistic (in love with self) and sees themselves as superiors to others.

You see a lot of vanity in professional athletes, actors, and those with high paying jobs who yield much power, prestige, and influence over others.

But beauty, wealth, and power mean nothing to God. To Him it is emptiness and worthless.

Mirrors can be harmful for they enable you to look in the mirror for hours idolizing your hair, face, body or clothes.

We are never to boast and be prideful of anything we possess. Remember, we don't own anything. Whatever you have are only temporary things that all belong to God. Material things and physical beauty will eventually fade.

Proverbs 31:30 *Charm is deceitful and beauty is vain, but a woman who fears the Lord, she shall be praised. (ESV)*

April 18

SHARING

When we were children we were taught to share with others. For some it was easy, and for others, it was not. Sharing is a recognized virtue in most civilized cultures because we understand instinctively that selfishness is wrong.

Whether you believe and follow God, you are still created in His image and are more like Him than any other created being.

Due to the sinful nature we all possess, we allow being selfish to rule instead of sharing. Beneath our phony smiles, our sinful hearts may be thinking, "What's mine is mine."

Christian sharing can take many different forms, but it is the heart attitude that matters to God. We will be more like Jesus when we freely share ourselves with those He brings into our lives.

So the next time you feel your self-holding back from sharing with someone, remember, Jesus shared everything with us----even His life.

Luke 3:11 *And he answered them, "Whoever has two shirts should share with him who has none, and whoever has food is to do likewise." (NIV)*

April 19

A CHILD IS A GIFT FROM GOD

From the beginning of time God speaks about the importance of children. Children are very important to God. They are a valuable part of God's Kingdom.

The disciples came to Jesus and asked, "Who, then, is the greatest in the Kingdom of Heaven?"

He answered, "Truly I tell you, unless you change and become like little children you will never enter the kingdom of Heaven."

Children are a blessing and God's greatest gift to man. Although raising children can be difficult, always remember what a blessing they are.

Be more child-like for they are God's perfect creation. Their spirits are filled with innocence, joy, and laughter. God tells us in scripture that we are His children and wants us to succeed and have a future of hope and success.

Love your child, no matter how old they are or how much grief they may bring.

***Isaiah* 49:15** *Can a mother forget the baby at her breast and have no compassion on the child she has borne? (NIV)*

April 20

ANIMALS ARE GOD SENT

Like children, animals are also precious gifts God has given to man. In the beginning, God gave man the authority over all that was created on earth. In Genesis 1 we find the creation of all things and see that God established the relationship between man and animal.

Man is to take care of animals --- not abuse them. In the beginning animals were used for food, but today they are used as man's greatest and loyal companion.

In one-way or another, nearly everybody's life is affected by animals. Because animals lack human abilities--- for they were not created in God's image, as man was--- does this mean they should be mistreated? No. The Bible indicates that God places a high value on animal life.

He approves his creation of animal and expects humans to treat them with due regard.

Proverbs 12:10: *A righteous man cares for the needs of his animal, but the kindest acts of the wicked are cruel. (NIV)*

April 21

PUTTING ONE FOOT IN FRONT OF THE OTHER

I am involved in every minute of your life. When I created you I mapped out every inch of your individual journey. Because sin was brought into the world, it has become a fallen world. This will bring problems in your life—some more severe than others.

Stay conscious of Me as you take each step, knowing I am there to pick you up when you trip. Put one foot carefully in front of the other so you don't fall.

As you trudge through the muddy waters, keep in mind there is a beautiful garden on the other side. The Holy Spirit will bring you to that place where there is peace and tranquility.

The light of my presence shines on you giving you the joy circumstances cannot.

Psalm 18:30 *As for God, His way is perfect; The Lord's word is flawless; He shields all who take refuge in Him. (NIV)*

April 22

WE ARE LIGHT WORKERS

I am the light in a world filled with darkness. Unlike a light bulb, my light never dies or fades, but remains bright and strong.

As my children, you are Light Workers. I instilled in you the power to light up peoples' worlds with kindness and love. In a world filled with hatred and turmoil you can be a role model to those who have not yet accepted to follow Me. Perhaps you can help guide them towards Me and to a better life.

Lead them up the mountain, as I have led you. Some of My richest blessings lie just beneath the top of the mountain. The higher you climb, the more spectacular the view becomes. I will eventually lead you down the other side of the mountain, into my dazzling light. Let my light continue to shine within you as you walk among those who are lost.

Psalm 107 *Oh give thanks to the Lord, for he is good, for his steadfast love endures forever. (ESV)*

◆ April 23 ◆

FAITH IS THE OPPOSITE OF DOUBT

Faith is belief with strong convictions—a firm belief in something for which there may be no tangible proof, complete trust, confidence, reliance, or devotion.

In other words, faith is the complete opposite of doubt. We have a hard time understanding something is real if we cannot see or touch it.

An example is God. He is invisible and nobody can see Him, but we know he is real.

The Bible tells us that God is incapable of lying and his integrity is perfect, therefore, when he declares the Bible to be true, we can accept that statement based on God's character.

Faith is trust, assurance, and confidence in God. If you find yourself questioning or doubting His existence, pray and ask Him to increase your faith.

Faith is only as strong as the things to which it is anchored. Faith is acting on the truth, whether we feel the truth or not, whether we like the truth or not, and whether we agree with the truth or not.

Hebrews 11 *Now faith is confidence in what we hope for and assurance about what we do not see. (NIV)*

April 24

PRAYER

What is prayer? Prayer is how we communicate with God. It is the way we get to know Him better.

Do you find yourself struggling to pray? Does praying seem like an exercise in an eloquent speech that you don't possess?

Do you go about saying the words but with no real meaning?

Prayer is not just reserved for the clergy and the religiously devout. Believers can pray from the heart in their own words.

There is no correct way to pray. Some people kneel down to pray, while others do it sitting in silence.

Think of prayer as a spiritual communication between man and God---a two-way relationship in which man should not only talk to God, but should listen to Him.

Prayer really works. God hears our prayers and responds to us because He is faithful and has compassion for His children.

Philippians 4:6-7 *Do not be anxious about anything, but in every situation, by prayer and petition, with thanksgiving let your requests be made known unto God. (NIV)*

April 25

"I'M AFRAID TO DIE!"

You are not alone! Many people are afraid to die. It is the unknown of not knowing what will happen to them or where they will go that frightens them. Many different religions believe that a person can come back in a different body, or return as an animal or plant.

Humans weren't originally created to experience death---they were created for life.

Death is a process that came as a result of sin.

Christians shouldn't fear death for death is not the end of the road for them. If our God defeated death, what do we have to fear?

Christians know they will go to Heaven to meet their creator. Heaven is Paradise designed to be the fulfillment of all we could ever want: Peace, worship, love, hope, fellowship, worship, and most of all constant face-to-face interaction with God.

So, there is no reason to fear death? It is merely one step closer to God.

Romans 10:9-10 *If you confess with your mouth "Jesus is Lord" and believe in your heart that God raised him from the dead, you will be saved. For it is with your heart that you believe and are justified, and it is with your mouth that you confess and are saved.* (CSB)

April 26

TEARS ARE A PART OF LIFE

Do not hold back tears. Dry your eyes and cry no more for I am your God. Some people cry when they are happy or sad, but I created you with the ability to cry, not only as an expression for your emotions, but also as an opportunity to release pent up feelings.

Tears are a part of life. We live in a fallen world where there is much to cry about--death, loss, disappointment.

Just as there is a time to cry, there is a time to stop crying. Do not grieve because as My child you have a hope within, through the presence of the Holy Spirit.

There are times to weep, but then wipe your tears and move forward in the faith. I am in control and make all things work together for your good.

Revelation 21:4 *And God shall wipe every tear from their eyes; and there shall be no more death, or mourning or crying or pain, for the ole order of things has passed away. (KJB)*

April 27

THE 7 DEADLY SINS

You have heard about "The 7 Deadly Sins" which are also called the capital sins. They are gluttony, envy, greed, lust, pride, sloth and wrath. In the Bible we are warned to stay away from these sins.

The first is lust. Lust is a strong passion or longing, especially for sexual desires. The next is gluttony, which is an excessive of eating or drinking. Third is Greed. Greed is an excessive pursuit of material things and the one sin that many people have trouble with.

Sloth is an excessive laziness. Wrath is a strong anger and hate towards another person. Envy is also something many people experience, for it is the intense desire to have an item that someone else has. And the last is pride. Pride is an excessive view of one's self. The Bible warns us not to boast and to be humble.

The 7 sins are abominations to God. Whenever you are confronted with one of these, pray to God for the willpower to overcome them and wait on Him to answer. The Bible makes clear that all sin leads to death; however we can be saved from sin and death through the ransom sacrifice of Jesus. He died for us so we can be set free.

Proverbs 6:16 *These six things doth the Lord hate: yea, seven are an abomination unto Him. (KJB)*

April 28

STRESS KILLS

Stress kills. Life often presents us with situations that are stressful that bring about worry, fear, and anxious. Stress brings on diseases such as cancer, stroke, and heart attacks.

Our culture is inundated with self-help books, psychiatrists, recovery programs, and stress related workshops.

We talk about simplifying our life, but most don't know how to accomplish that. Unfortunately, we don't know how to unload the stress we carry and try different ways, such as through the use of alcohol, drugs, and gambling.

When you feel overloaded and stressed, take a deep breath and call my name. Ask me to take away your worries. I will calm you and fill you with peace.

Matthew 11:28-30 *Come to me all you who are weary and burdened and I will give you rest. (NIV)*

April 29

GROWING OLD

Nobody looks forward to growing old. Growing old means slowing down, painful joints, and wrinkled skin. But the Bible presents growing old as a normal, natural part of life. As humans we are born with a tendency to "live for the moment," but as soon as we see our skin wrinkle we run to the plastic surgeon.

Old age is a blessing from the Lord. We should not be afraid of aging. Old age brings wisdom, and the more years we live, the more experiences we're given to learn from.

Some of us fear growing older for physical reasons. Aging is often seen as a loss of control. Maybe our bodies aren't able to do what they once could and our memories aren't as sharp.

What does God say about growing old? If we listen to the One who created us, we will hear about grace and goodness; not fear and resistance. He reminds us more than once in His word that growing older is an honor.

Psalms 71:9 *Cast me not off in the time of old age; forsake me not when my strength fails. (KJV)*

April 30

THE PURSUIT OF HAPPINESS

Everyone wants to be happy, but most are unable to find it. The Bible says happiness is a byproduct of Loving God.

When happiness becomes our singular aim without a desire to please God, evil is sure to follow. Sin always puts 'self' first, and when 'self' is first it will keep itself there, until you turn to Jesus and make Him first.

All men, whether they believe in their Creator or not, seek to live out the idea that they are endowed by their Creator with certain unalienable rights. Among these are life, liberty, and the pursuit of happiness. But when the Creator becomes our Father, how we pursue happiness will be different. True and lasting happiness is found in God alone, through Jesus Christ alone.

Psalm 37:4-14 *Take delight in the Lord and he will give you the desires of the heart. (NIV)*

MAY

May 1

QUIT TRYING TO PLAN THINGS

We try to plan things in our life, such as when we will marry, have children, or where we will go on vacation the next year. When our plans don't work out, we blame it on other people or circumstances.

But we are not in control of things--- God is. He probably sits up there laughing when we try to do things our way saying, "I'll just let her try to do it her way," and when we mess up, we get frustrated and angry.

Everything that happens in your life is *supposed* to happen and *exactly* the way it does. There are no surprises or coincidences. God is in control of everything--- so let go. It will be so much easier when you learn to give everything to God.

2 Timothy 1:7 *For God gave us a spirit not of fear, but of power and love and self-control. (ESV)*

May 2

TAKE TIME TO SMELL THE ROSES

In this fast, crazy world it is hard to relax. 'Taking time to Smell the Roses' is moot. Hustle, bustle and running around with your head cut off are everyday occurrences in most peoples' lives.

Everyone needs to relax and rest. The Bible speaks quite highly of rest. It is a repeated theme throughout Scripture, beginning with the creation week. God created for six days, then he rested. To rest, we have to trust that God will take care of things for us.

For the Christian, the ultimate rest is found in Christ. It is only in Him that we find our complete rest from the labors of our self-effort. We can now cease from our worries and troubles and rest in Him, not just one day or one week, but always.

Try to take time and smell the roses----time is running out.

Matthew 11:28-30 *Come to me, all who labor and are heavy laden, and I will give you rest. Take my yoke upon you, and learn from me, for I am gentle and lowly in heart, and you will find rest for your souls. For my yoke is easy, and my burden is light. (NIV)*

May 3

WHY GOD ALLOWS SUFFERING

There is nothing sadder than seeing a child suffer. We often ask God why he allows this? In the Bible it describes numerous times when God brought plagues and diseases on both his people and his enemies. It says he did it, "to make you see my power."

It's hard to imagine our loving and merciful God displaying such wrath and anger toward His children. But God's punishments always have the goal of repentance and restoration.

Whether disease is part of God's judgment, the result of living in a fallen, sinful world, and whether or not it's a sign that the end of the time is beginning, our response should be the same. Without the saving blood of Christ shed for us, we will pay for our sins for all eternity in a hell that will make the worst pandemic seem mild.

But for the Christian we have the assurance of salvation and the hope of eternity because Christ suffered on the cross for us.

God allows us to suffer to turn us away from the world toward greater hope in the life to come.

Jeremiah 33:6 *Behold, I will bring to it health and healing, and I will heal them and reveal to them abundance of prosperity and security. (KJV)*

May 4

INFEDELITY

Today 1 out of 2 marriages will end in divorce. There are many reasons for this, such as monetary problems or infidelity.

One of the biggest reasons for divorce is infidelity. Infidelity is devastating to a marriage. There are many reasons why sex occurs outside of marriage. Some people get trapped into having an affair to give a conscious or subconscious "wake up call" to their spouse.

Another reason is because some people get wrapped up in an affair to inflate their ego because their spouse quit complimenting or paying attention to them.

Infidelity is one of the most frequently condemned sins in the Bible. Adultery is mentioned 52 times; including The Ten Commandments, all 4 Gospels, and 10 other books of the Bible.

Only the sins of idolatry, self-righteousness, and murder are mentioned more often.

While there are a number of reasons for infidelity, the majority of cases occur because of a need to be emotionally connected.

It is important to remember that marital infidelity, like all sins, can be forgiven. While forgiving and forgetting is not instinctive or easy, God's grace is always sufficient.

Corinthians 6:18 *Flee from sexual immorality. All other sins a person commits are outside the body, but whoever sins sexually, sins against their own body. (NIV)*

May 5

WHAT WILL HEAVEN LOOK LIKE?

What does the Bible say that Heaven looks like? Are there angels playing harps, or animals frolicking through the clouds?

Heaven exists today, although humans are unable to see it.

The pictures that we have seen cannot even begin to describe it accurately in all its beauty and splendor.

In the Bible there are actually 3 heavens described. The first is called firmament--- or sky that covers the earth. The second is where the stars, the sun, and the moon reside. It is the space beyond the earth and it covers the entire universe.

The third heaven is the home of God and Jesus Christ. This is where the dead martyrs and saints are.

Sounds wonderful, doesn't it? Well, the only way for you to see heaven is through the Son of God, Jesus Christ. If you have not declared that Jesus Christ is your Lord, it is not too late.

Heaven is your eternal home. Your reward is awaiting you.

Revelation 21:1-2 *Then I saw a new Heaven and a new earth, for the first heaven and the first earth had passed away, and there was no longer any sea. I saw the Holy City, the New Jerusalem, coming down out of heaven from God, prepared as a bride beautifully dressed for her husband. (NIV)*

May 6

AGE WITH GRACE

Some people talk of old age as the "Golden Years," but unfortunately, for most people, they are not so golden. With age comes pain, disease and for some, poverty.

The human body was never designed to live forever, and we will advance through these stages as we proceed toward the end of our lives.

It is important to keep a positive, even humorous perspective on aging, because God designed our bodies to age. Age should bring a level of maturity and mellowing gained by experience.

God planned a wonderful future beyond any certainty of growing old and ending our days on earth. With faith we can find there really is gold to be found in The Golden Years, for what is waiting for us when we die is worth more than all the gold in the world!

Psalms 90:10 *The days of our years are threescore years and ten; and if by reason of strength they be fourscore years; yet is their strength labor and sorrow for it is soon cut off, and we fly away. (KJV)*

May 7

GOD'S PLAN FOR YOU

"But I'm a Christian. Why do I still have pain and disease?" Many Christians question God and ask him this.

The world is in a sin-filled state and sin causes disease. We live stress lived lives, refuse to forgive others, and refuse to ask God to forgive us when we sin.

God heals, but healing is not always the only path that He chooses for us. Sometimes His perfect plan for our lives is to allow us to suffer and experience disease, illness, and hardship.

God strengthens us, molds us, and builds us through hardship. We must realize that sometimes its just not God's plan to heal or fix a problem quickly for us.

But He still loves us and has a profound purpose for that pain that can end up blessing us beyond anything we could ever imagine.

So the next time you are in pain, don't question God, but thank Him for He is drawing you closer to him.

James 5-13 *Is anyone among you suffering? Let him pray. Is anyone cheerful? Let him sing.* (ESV)

May 8

ANGELS ARE REAL

Are angels real? Are they truly around us? The truth is angels walk among us. Angels are spiritual beings with a much different frequency compared to humans.

Angels are an entirely different order of being than humans. Human beings do not become angels after they die and angels will never become human beings.

Early versions of angels had no gender, though many photos later showed angels as tall slender males, usually with long blond hair, soft features and often dressed in flowing robes. The angels most people are familiar with today are the Christian angels that originated from the Hebrew Testaments.

Though angels are said to dwell in heaven, their visits to the earthly realm are not always benevolent. According to the Bible there are armies: like warrior angels, angels of death, and so on. They are mentioned almost 300 times in Scripture. They not only minister and lead us, but they protect us.

Angels are simply messengers and protectors dispensed from God. We are all assigned our own personal angel, called a Guardian Angel as Hebrews 1:14 indicates. (*Are not all angels ministering spirits sent to serve those who will inherit salvation?)

Embrace your angel and give thanks to God for sending him.

Colossians 1:16 *For in him all things were created: things in heaven and on earth, visible and invisibles, whether thrones or powers or rulers or authorities; all things have been created through him and for him. (NIV)*

May 9

SHARING WEALTH

It costs a lot of money to support a family today. Many families require both parents to work just to make ends meet. The cost of living seems to grow higher and higher every year, while paychecks don't climb nearly as quickly.

Did you know that in Jesus' time it was a common belief that great wealth was a sign of God's favor and poverty was God's punishment for sin?

However, Jesus denied that wealth is a sign of God's favor, or that poverty is God's punishment for sin.

Wealth is a gift from God to be used in His service. Those who have been blessed with wealth must share generously with the poor and avoid the sins of arrogance and greed.

Those blessed with wealth beyond his need have a responsibility to share generously with the less fortunate. It is not the wealth that is intrinsically evil or that poverty is blessed, rather a devotion to gathering wealth is incompatible with devotion to God. God must always be the most important thing in your life.

Luke 16:13 *No one can serve two masters: for either he will hate one and love the other, or be devoted to one and despise the other. You cannot serve both God and money.* (NIV)

May 10

MARRIAGE

The Bible states that God created man and then made woman to complement him. It is God's "fix," for the fact that it is not good for the man to be alone.

In fact, the Bible says that God performed the very first marriage on the sixth day of Creation week. It's important to note that God initiated this very first marriage in the Garden of Eden.

Marriage comes from God. In order for a marriage to be solid, both the husband and wife have to be believers. If one is and the other is not, the marriage will not survive.

Marriage is an intimate and complementing union between a man and a woman in which the two become one physically, in the whole life.

Today, marriage is taken for granted and there are far too many divorces. This saddens God for He created this blessed union, and mankind has ignored His wishes.

If you are in a marriage and there are signs of trouble, pray to God to help. Do not fall weak to the temptations of the enemy.

Mark 10:6-9 *But at the beginning of creation God 'made them male and female.'* (NIV)

May 11

HE WILL SET THE WORLD RIGHT

God is gracious and good so why does He allow Christians to suffer? Many are suffering physically, financially, spiritually and emotionally.

How can He allow such things in His world such as war, broke homes, diseases, pain and death----especially when their effects often are felt most keenly by those who are apparently innocent?

When man looks through the eyes of circumstance his conclusion will be born from his vain imagination. Every question man poses, he can find the answer in God's word.

We are conditioned to seek for ways in which we can profit spiritually from the sufferings in life, as well as the blessings.

The world is now under God's curse because of man's rebellion against God's commands. God did not create the world this way and one day He will set all things right again.

Be patient in trying times and remember Romans 8:28. "*All things work together for good to those who love God.*" *(KJV)*

Revelation 21:4 *And God shall wipe away all tears from their eyes and there shall be not more death, neither sorrow, nor crying, neither shall there be any more pain; for the former things are passed away. (KJV)*

May 12

YOUR LIFE'S PURPOSE

We ask ourselves, "What is our purpose in life?"

What does the Bible say about life's purpose? The Bible affirms human purpose in two ways. First, there is a general purposefulness about human life. Second, there is also individual purpose in life.

A purpose that applies to all humans is that of knowing and enjoying God. Individually, God has purposes for our lives. There are universal good works prepared for us---such as obedience to Christ and witnessing and enjoying God.

God made no two men alike. He created us to be unique. Beliefs about God's plans for our individual lives vary. God has a purpose for our lives.

To find out your purpose—pray and listen to what He says. He will not direct you to do something contrary to His character or His word. Finding purpose in your life is the greatest human quest.

Thankfully, believers can rest in the fact that their lives do have purpose. He knows His plans for you; He desires that we know him, and that we live out our unique role in his body.

Psalm 139: 13 *For you created my inmost being; you knit me together in my mother's womb. (NIV)*

May 13

AND GOD CREATED WOMAN

God created women to be the most incredible balance of soft and strong. And we have the incredible ability to be so many different things to so many different people.

If you have good thoughts, they will shine out of your face like sunbeams and you will look brilliant.

Every woman has inside her a piece of good news. The news is that you don't know great you can be, how much you can love, what you can accomplish, and what your potential is.

1 Corinthians 15:10 *By the grace of God, I am, I am what I am.* (KJV)

May 14

THE IDEAL WOMAN

One of the definitions of beauty in the dictionary is "a beautiful person, especially a woman."

When man thinks of beauty he thinks of a woman. The Bible has much to say about the beauty of women.

In Proverbs 31 we see an entire chapter devoted to what King Lenuel's mother taught him about the ideal woman. She taught him to look for something beautiful in the woman that he would have for his wife because God made all women to be something beautiful.

A woman can be beautiful on the outside, but ugly on the inside. Make sure your beauty comes from within.

Proverbs 31:10 *An excellent wife who can find? She is far more precious than jewels. (ESV)*

May 15

CHANGE IS DIFFICULT

One thing that can be difficult is change. How many times have you seen in your life or someone else's that an event can change their entire life? It can happen in the blink of an eye. Whether it is because of an illness, financial situations or relationship--- while change can be disconcerting or upsetting, change is necessary.

You have to have faith and know that whatever the situation is, God is in control. He is the ONLY thing that never changes. He is in control of your life, he loves you, and has a beautiful plan for you. Enjoy the journey!

Jeremiah 29:11 *For I know the plans I have for you", declares the Lord, "plans for welfare and nor for evil, to give you a future and a hope. (ESV)*

May 16

THINK LIKE A QUEEN!

A woman is like a tea bag. You can't tell how strong she is until she gets put in hot water. A woman's beauty comes from so many more places than her outer appearance. The list of female strengths is endless. Women provide the foundation of power, grace, wisdom, justice, creativity and hope.

They are known to have better intuition, patience, emotional focus and compassion. A strong woman is one who feels deeply and loves fiercely. Her tears flow just as abundantly as he laughter. A strong woman in her essence is a gift to the world.

Proverbs 31:25 *She is clothed with strength and dignity, and she laughs without fear of the future. (NLT)*

May 17

DO NOT YIELD TO TEMPTATIONS

Temptations are part of everyday life. They are inevitable; yet many Christians yield to temptations. There will always be temptations vying for our hearts. Sometimes they are subtle, and sometimes they are more obvious.

Though we are not free from temptation, we are free from the bondage it breeds. Christians who are perpetually discouraged are the most difficult to influence for the glory of God and the furtherance of the Gospel of Jesus Christ.

The key to overcoming temptation is the reality and reliability of God's word. The Holy Spirit will never direct us contrary to the Word of God.

Knowing the fact that Jesus Christ is our Shepherd will keep us from over-reacting to over-whelming pressure in a superficial way.

Corinthians 10:13 *No temptation has overtaken you that is not common to man. God is faithful and he will not let you be tempted beyond your ability, but with the temptation he will also provide the way of escape, that you may be able to endure it. (NIV)*

May 18

PRESSURE ON CHRISTIANS

It happens! God will put pressure on Christians.

But why? He will apply pressure with the intent of bringing about repentance and a renewed confidence and contentment with his perfect will.

When a believer leans to their own understanding, they are certain to suffer disillusionment. When we really see ourselves as the Lord see us, it is not the terribly offensive sins of the flesh that shock us, but the awful nature of the pride of our own hearts opposing Jesus Christ.

When you are faced with the question of whether or not to open and surrender your heart-- make a determination to go through whatever pressure God has permitted. You will take great pleasure in knowing you are not alone.

James 1:12 *Blessed is the man who remains steadfast under trial, for when he has stood the test he will receive the crown of life, which God promised to those who love Him. (ESV)*

May 19

FASTING

To many Christians prayer is not enough, so they choose to fast. If you decide to fast, is it for spiritual renewal, for guidance, or what reason?

Ask the Holy Spirit to clarify His leading and objectives for your prayer fast.

Fasting requires reasonable precautions physically. If you are taking medication, consult your physician first. If this is your first time, start out slowly. First fast one meal, and gradually work up to a 48-hour fast. Ideally, fasting should begin in the evening.

The key to fasting is repentance. Jesus instructed that all of His followers should fast. *(Matthew 6:16-18 "When you fast, do not look somber as the hyprocrites do, for they disfigure their faces to show others they are fasting. NIV)*

For Christ, it was a matter of when believers would fast, not if they would. Just this statement alone from the Lord is sufficient reason why we should make fasting a matter of routine.

Luke 5:33-39 *They said to him, "John's disciples often fast and pray, and so do the disciples of the Pharisees, but yours go on eating and drinking." (NIV)*

May 20

BE WILLING TO BEND FOR OTHERS

Do you consider yourself a strong person? Not physically, but spiritually and emotionally. Some people see rigidness as being strong. These people live in a box and live by the rules. They are usually not acceptable of those who do not live inside the box, too.

Others are more flexible. This type of person is the stronger of the two because they have more opportunities to build a relationship with those who have a different mindset.

You can't share your faith walk with people you do not have relationships with. Be willing to bend in order to be strong.

Isaiah 33:2 *Lord, be gracious to us; we long for you. Be our strength every morning and our salvation in time of distress. (NIV)*

May 21

LEARNING TO TRUST IN GOD

Oh, ye woman of little faith. Why do you worry? Worry isn't necessary because you only need to trust in God. God is a great privilege and comfort for the believer.

But how many of you say, the "I trust God" words while still worrying. How do you make the transition from worrying to completely trusting in the Lord?

The next time you have an issue that causes you to worry, give it to God. Tell him you are giving the issue to Him and trust in Him completely. Learning to trust God is something you have to work on. It is a journey.

Isaiah 26:3 *You will keep in perfect peace those whose minds are steadfast, because they trust in you. (NIV)*

May 22

CRYING IS HEALTHY

Crying does not mean you are weak. No, it's just the opposite. I created tears to help you vent on certain situations, vent your emotions, and relieving pressure that lies inside.

While crying cannot fix your problems, tears clear away the stresses that make your viewpoint and thinking process cloudy.

There are different types of tears. Emotional tears are tears that begin in the cerebrum which register sadness and happiness. Basal tears keep our eyes wet, and reflex tears form in response to an irritant.

Tears are a cleansing to our body as soap is. They do a wonderful job of relieving pressure, so next time you feel tears swelling up, let them flow.

Psalm 147: 3 *He heals the brokenhearted and binds up their wounds. (NIV)*

May 23

ONE DAY AT A TIME

Trust me one day at a time. This keeps you close to me and responsive to my will. Trust is not a natural response--- especially for those who have been deeply wounded. My spirit within you is your resident tutor, helping you in this supernatural endeavor. Yield to me and be sensitive to my prompting.

You find yourself wandering at times. Your mind goes in all directions. Don't let your need to understand distract you from me. I will help you get through the day if you yield to me and depend on Me, and Me alone.

Trust me one day at a time and one minute at a time.

Psalm 84: 12 *Lord Almighty, blessed is the one who trusts in you. (NIV)*

May 24

THE PRAYER ROOM

You are being weighed down by an abundance of problems.

They require more and more of your attention--- but do not give in to them. Whenever it feels like you are going to explode, go into your personal Prayer Room and close the door.

Humbly bring me your prayers and petitions. Your problems will dissipate when you see them in the Light of My Presence. You need to remember who I am and how much I love you.

These problems are fleeting. No matter how big the mountain may seem, remember---- This Too Shall Pass!

Exodus 3:14 *God said to Moses, "I AM WHO I AM. Say this to the people of Israel: I am has sent me to you."* (KJV)

May 25

A BELIEVER MARRYING AN UNBELIEVER

It is said that a believer should not marry an unbeliever. When God permits a Christian to marry an unbeliever He will use the unbeliever to chastise the Christian with the express purpose of bringing spiritual growth for the Believer and redemption of the unbeliever.

Once the Christian and the unbeliever are bound in marriage it is God's will for that marriage to remain until death do them part. There is nothing more attractive to Christ than a Christian who is perpetually influenced by the grace of God.

If you are married to an unbeliever, it is your duty to lead him to the Lord. That is why God has allowed you to join together.

1 Peter 3 *Wives, in the same way submit yourselves to your own husbands so that, if any of them do not believe the word, they may be won over without words by the behavior of their wives. (NIV)*

May 26

RELATIONSHIPS

We are aware of the importance of relationships. Our family and friendships are very important to us. It's good to know that someone is walking with you through life.

At times it is good for someone to hold your hand and pray with you---even to cry with you. When two people share an emotion, it is better. If it is sad, sharing the situation has less power, but if it is happy, shared joy has double the happiness.

Thank me for the people in your life who share the joys and sorrows. Thank them for being there. You can be the person who needs someone. Open your heart to let someone else's sorrow or joy in.

Ecclesiates 4:9-10 *Two are better than one, because they have a good return for their labor. If either of them falls down, one can help the other up. But pity anyone who falls and has no one to help them up. (NIV)*

May 27

SELF-PITY

Self-pity is a bottomless pit. Once you fall in you find yourself going deeper and deeper. On the way down you will find yourself wallowing in sorrow and depression.

Everyone is prone to self-pity for we are human and are born self-centered and proud. We feel we are entitled to things and when we don't get them, we find ourselves slipping down the pit.

Self-pity causes us to sulk. You may find yourself getting mad at God, but remember, self-pity is not God, but self. Any time we are focused on ourselves we are in the territory of the flesh.

When we surrender our lives to Christ, our old nature is crucified with Him. When self is dominant--God is not.

Romans 8:7 *For the mind that is set on the flesh is hostile to God, for it does not submit to God's law. (NIV)*

May 28

BE THANKFUL FOR EVERYTHING

A thankful attitude opens the doors to Heaven and my blessings will fall freely on you. Although you cannot be here with me yet for it is not yet your time, you can catch glimpses of what it will be like to live with me.

Being thankful for everything is the language of love. A thankful heart and mind rejoices in me. I am your refuge and strength.

Thankfulness is a prominent Bible theme. It should be a way of life for us, naturally flowing from our hearts and mouths. We should be thankful, because God is worthy of our thanksgiving.

Expressing thankfulness helps us remember that God is in control and healthy and beneficial to us.

Ephesians 1:3 *Blessed be the God the Father of our Lord Jesus Christ, who has blessed us in Christ with every spiritual blessing in the heavenly places. (NLT)*

May 29

DEALING WITH PRESSURE

Do you feel you are under pressure? You are not alone. We often make decisions that leave us vulnerable to worldly influences. It is during these times that God will apply pressure with the intent of bringing about repentance and a renewed confidence with His perfect will.

Many of us want to solve the problem on our own, which is the opposite of what God wants, ultimately resulting in a sense of futility. Thus, we weaken ourselves because we will not trust and obey God. It is for this reason that God applies pressure in our lives.

Unless we experience the pressure of facing every deception about ourselves, we will claw to the depths of our hearts before we give the Holy Spirit our consideration.

James 1: 12 *Blessed is the man who remains steadfast under trail, for when he stood the test he will receive the crown of life, which God has promised to those who love him. (ESV)*

May 30

LIVING A FULFILLING LIFE

Everyone wants to be happy and live a calm and peaceful life. But that's not the way it is. With all the sin and temptations in the world today, we find ourselves living in turmoil, anxiety, and fear.

From the moment we are born we recognize an insatiable hunger for wanting more out of life. We try to enjoy every relationship and maximize every opportunity. As we try to fill our lives we can never be fully satisfied. The desire to live, rather then exist, is what separates humans from animals.

If we were created by God himself to live a fulfilling life, why do so many of us feel like we are running on empty? Though we were created to live lives that are rich and satisfying, they can only be complete by having a relationship with Jesus. When we expect to live completely fulfilling lives without God, we expect something of life that it was never designed to give.

John 16:33 *I have said these things to you, that in me you may have peace. In the world you will have tribulation. But take heart: I have overcome the world.* (NIV)

May 31

L-O-V-E

What is love? How do we define it? The American Heritage Dictionary defines love as "an intense affection for another person based on familial or personal ties."

We love based on feelings and emotions that can change from one moment to the next. We have different types of love: love for another person, or an animal. But the Bible tells us "God is love." *(1 John 4:8 The one who does not love has not become acquainted with God, for God is love. NIV)*

One way God defines love is in the act of giving. After all, God sacrifices His only Son so that we, who put faith in His son, will not spend eternity separated from him.

God's love is very different than human love. It is unconditional and not based on feelings or emotions. He doesn't love us because we are lovable or we make Him feel good. He loves us because He is love.

Isn't that enough for you?

John 3:16 *For God so loved the world, that he gave his only begotten Son, that whosoever believeth in him should not perish, but have everlasting life. (KJV)*

JUNE

June 1

THE WONDERS OF A SIMPLE SMILE

Something as simple as a smile can change a persons' life. There is a connection that happens when one person smiles at another. It is an acknowledgment that says, "You are someone and I'm glad I have met you.

A smile is kind and caring and the first step you take in sharing God's love with someone.

A smile is a universal welcome remark. It is a symbol that is rated with having the highest positive emotional content. Everyone's smile is unique and their own. When your brain feels happy, you smile. It reduces stress and generates more positive emotions in you.

And the best thing is that smiling is free! There's magic in a smile--- so the next time you come face to face with someone---smile! It is the sunshine that God gave you to share with another.

1 Thessalonians 3:12 *May the Lord cause you to increase and overflow in love for each other and for everyone else, just as we also do for you. (NIV)*

June 2

WHY THERE IS DISEASE IN THE WORLD

The world is full of disease. There are spiritual causes that are behind these genetic, environmental causes. Some people ask why God allows disease. One of the main causes of illness is sin.

Sin was caused by our first parents Adam and Eve.

The history of the human race is the story of the endless struggle against disease. Medicine, money, and research alone cannot win the battle of disease.

Perhaps it is time to ask, "Why have we failed to win the battle against disease?" Did a loving and perfect Creator reveal fundamental concepts that would revolutionize our approach to health?

The Bible states that "The fear of the Lord is the beginning of knowledge" *(Proverbs 1:7 NIV)* When we look at Scripture for instructions about health, it is remarkable what our Creator has revealed.

God said, "We could avoid the curse of disease if we obeyed His commandments and statutes." *(Exodus 15:26 RSVA)*

Anyone brave enough to examine the Bible will find that it challenges assumptions that have blinded generations and can play a vital role in defeating disease!

Exodus 23:35 *You shall serve the Lord your God and he will bless your bread and water and I will take sickness away from among you. (ESV)*

June 3

LIFE IS A SONG, GAME, DREAM, CHALLENGE, LOVE AND SACRIFICE

When you learn not to get anxious and fret about everything—especially things you can't do anything about—your life will be more peaceful, happier, and you will be able to enjoy the gift of life that our Father has given us.

Life is a song, so sing it, even if you have a non-melodic voice. Life is a game, so play it.

Life is a challenge—confront it with prayer and faith.

Life is a dream—realize it and make it the most colorful and happy life you can.

Life is a sacrifice, so offer it to our Father in Heaven as he sacrificed his life for us.

And most of all, life is love—enjoy it! Enjoy everything, even when times are not good, for remember—this too shall pass. Enjoy everything, everyday, from the moment your eyes open in the morning until you close them at night.

John 6:35 *Jesus said to them, "I am the bread of life; whoever comes to me shall not hunger, and whoever believes in me shall never thirst."* (ESV)

June 4

THE THREE PHASES OF LIFE

In life there are three phases: The past, the present and the future. The past is where many of us tend to get stuck in. It's like being stuck in quicksand and you can't get out.

Whether its due to a regret you may have from a broken relationship or marriage, or you are a victim of "should have, could have and should have's," you will never be able to enjoy "the present," if you are consumed in "the past."

Unfortunately, we are all products of our past, but we don't have to be prisoners of it. Let go of it now and enjoy the present for that is exactly what it is from God.

Philippians 3:13 *Brothers and sisters, I do not consider myself yet to have taken hold of it. But one thing I do: Forgetting what is behind and straining toward what is ahead. (NIV)*

June 5

THE DIFFERENCE BETWEEN RELIGIOUS AND SPIRITUAL

Many people are religious and not spiritual and vice versa. What is the difference between being spiritual and being religious?

Spirituality is the quality of being concerned with the human spirit or soul, as opposed to material or physical things. Religion implies a belief in and worship of a superhuman controlling power.

A spiritual person grows from the inside out. This is not something you can go to a school to learn. The only way to be spiritual is to be your own teacher, for there is no one other than yourself who can teach you, but your own soul.

John 14:17 *Even the spirit of truth, whom the world cannot receive, because it neither sees him nor knows him. You know him, for he dwells with you and he will be in you. (KJV)*

June 6

OUR GUARDIAN ANGEL

It is said we all are assigned 'our own special angel' in life. So are angels real? Are they the ones who help us in situations when something happens in our lives and there is no valid reasonable explanation of how we may have survived the situation?

People have told stories where they lost control of a vehicle and miraculously survived without a scratch. Some have said that they felt like someone or something was there with them at the time, but when they looked there was no one.

Yes, angels are real and visit us during our life. We don't hear the rustle of the wings, nor feel the feathery touch of the breast of a dove, but you will know their presence by the love they create in our hearts and peace in our souls.

Hebrews 1:14 *Are not all angels ministering spirits sent to those who will inherit salvation? (NIV)*

June 7

THE ACT OF GIVING

The best feeling you can have is to give to someone. It doesn't have to be an expensive gift-- it could be something as simple as a smile or a hug.

Giving is wonderfully simple and imaginably complex, all at the same time. We give to others so we can bless ourselves.

Each and every day, do something for someone else, for by doing this you will get a feeling that money can't buy. You have not lived today until you have done something for someone else who can never repay you.

An example in the Bible is in Genesis 14: 19-20, when Abram gives Melchizedek a tenth of his spoils, but there is no command to do so. Everything we own and have comes from God. So when we give, we simply offer Him a small portion of the abundance He has already given to us.

Acts 20:35 *In all things I have shown you that by working hard in this way we must help the weak and remember the words of the Lord Jesus, how he himself said, "it is more blessed to give than to receive". (ESV)*

June 8

FOCUS ON POSITIVE THINGS

Unfortunately, many people enjoy listening to the negative stories and situations that occur in our world. The news is mostly about murders, scandals, and derogatory things. The media only writes about such things for it appears to be the 'norm.'

But remember a tree that falls makes more noise than a forest that grows.

Try to focus on positive things in your life and steer away from people who are negative and bring you down. A flower blooms with sunlight and water, not cold and darkness.

Hebrews 13:5 *Keep your lives free from the love of money and be content with what you have for he said, "I will never leave you nor forsake you."* (NIV)

June 9

THE SECRET OF GOOD HEALTH

The secret of good health for both your body and your mind is easy. Do not mourn and dwell in the past, nor worry about what the future holds—but live in the moment wisely and earnestly.

True happiness can only be achieved by looking inward and learning to enjoy whatever life has given you, and this requires transforming greed into gratitude.

As Proverbs 17:22 teaches---*A merry heart doeth good like a medicine; but a broken spirit drieth the bones. (KJV)*

Philippians 4:11-13 *Not that I speak from want: for I have learned, in whatsoever state I am, therewith to be content. (ESV)*

June 10

DO NOT CARE WHAT PEOPLE THINK

If you care about what others think of you---you will be their prisoner. Remember the old adage our mothers used to tell us, "Sticks and stones can break your bones, but names will never harm you."

This is true, for you can not be loved by everyone. There will always be someone who will be jealous or envious and try to hurt you in some way.

When you find yourself in this type of situation, let it go. It will pass. Be a bigger and better person and do not retaliate and lower yourself to their level.

Find it in your heart to smile and pray for them. Jesus was mocked and betrayed by one of His own apostles and crucified for declaring He was the Son of God. But He forgave him for it was in Gods plan, in order to bring man back to God.

Luke 23:34 *Then Jesus said, "Father, forgive them, for they do not know what they are doing."* (NIV)

June 11

IT'S TOUGH BEING AN ADULT

Being an adult can be trying at times. We have a big responsibility—supporting others, working, taking care of our homes and family, and confronted with any crisis that may occur.

When we are small we can't wait until we are adults so we can enjoy the things only adults can do, such as driving, voting and drinking alcohol. When we were children we had fun, were spontaneous, and filled with joy. Now that we are grown we deal with problems on a daily basis.

Joy should be a part of life even for grown-ups because our Father, God, created a wonderful beautiful world for us to live in. Even though you may have unpleasant situations in your life at the time, remember, it is only temporary. Every single thing does not have to be serious. Loosen up and have some fun.

Philippians 4:6-9 *Be careful for nothing; but in every thing by prayer and supplication with thanksgiving let your requests be made unto God. (KJB)*

June 12

IT'S UP TO YOU TO BE OK

The same boiling water that softens the potato hardens the egg. It's all about what you are made of—not the circumstances.

It's OK not to be OK.

It's just as easy being a kind and compassionate person than one who criticizes and judges. Love yourself, accept yourself and be good to yourself, because without you the rest of the world would be without a source of many wonderful things.

James 5:16 *Therefore, confess your sins to one another and pray for one another, that you may be healed. The prayer of a righteous person has great power as it is working. (ESV)*

June 13

ACCEPT WHAT IT IS, LET GO OF WHAT IT WAS, AND HAVE FAITH IN WHAT WILL BE.

We are all insecure to a point, and there is nothing wrong in that. The problem arises when we try to counter this insecurity by cultivating this illusion of control and start taking ourselves and everybody else too seriously.

It can take a lot of practice to relax around things that are not good for you, but it's worth doing! Learn to say, "I can be happy not with this or because of this, but in spite of this!"

Romans 8:28 *And we know that for those who love God all things work together for good, for those who are called according to his purpose. (KJV)*

June 14

LOVE EVERYONE, BUT BE CAUTIOUS

Love all, but trust few. Learn to love without condition, talk without bad intention, give without reason, and most of all care for people without expectation.

If you expect less than what you think you deserve, you will never be disappointed.

Being careful isn't a bad thing. It's hard not to try to block yourself from feeling strongly about others when things haven't worked out in the past. Find the balance. With unparalleled pain also comes unparalleled joy.

Proverbs 10:28 *The hope of the righteous brings joy, but the expectation of the wicked will perish. (ESV)*

June 15

ONE SMALL ACT CAN MAKE THE DIFFERENCE

If you see someone falling behind, walk beside him. If you see someone being ignored, find a way to include him. If someone has been knocked down, lift him up. Always remind people how important they are. One small act could mean the world to them.

We are living in a "Me First" type of society. We are self-focused and self-possessed.

You never know what another person is truly going through.

A small random act of kindness can change a life and change the world! When you perform an act of kindness, it has a domino effect.

There is a healing power of kindness that is amazing.

Proverbs 19:17 *Whoever is generous to the poor lends to the Lord, and he will repay him for his deed. (ESV)*

June 16

HOW TO WIN A SPIRITUAL BATTLE

15 Simple truths to repeat when you are in a spiritual battle:

1) God's got this
2) The Lord fights for me
3) Jesus loves me
4) Not today, Satan!
5) It is finished
6) His grace is sufficient
7) I am not alone
8) I am fearfully and wonderfully made
9) Fear has no grip on me
10) Christ is enough for me
11) He has overcome the world
12) I am a new creation in Christ
13) Sin doesn't define me---Christ does
14) Be still and know
15) God is good

Practicing, acting out, and believing in the steps above will make you victorious and defeat the enemy.

Ephesians 6:11 *Put on the whole armor of God, that you may be able to stand against the schemes of the devil. (ESV)*

June 17

TWO GIFTS FROM GOD

God gives us two gifts each and every day: One is a choice the other is a chance.

The choice of a good life and the chance to make it the best you can! It is up to you in which way to go.

God gives us second chances. Because we are imperfect, we make mistakes, yet through our moments of imperfection, we are humbled with the realization of God's grace and mercy as He forgives us.

Our Father also gives us choices. He gave Eve a choice and she failed. Because of this, the world is full of sin. God gives us choices and the consequences of some we make are more deadly than others.

The next time you have to make a choice---stop and think. We may all get away with sinning for a while---however, in time we will reap what we have sown.

Proverbs 14:12 *There is a way that seems right to a man, but its end is the way to death. (BSB)*

June 18

WE ARE ACCOUNTABLE FOR OUR ACTIONS

Do not be impressed by money, social status, or a job title. Be impressed by the way someone treats other human beings. The Bible has a lot to say about money, wealth, greed and contentment.

We are accountable to God for how we use everything He gives us in this life, including money. Saving money demonstrates good stewardship of the resources God gives us.

Proverbs 23:4-5 *Do not wear yourself out to get rich; do not trust your own cleverness. Cast but a glance at riches and they are gone for they will surely sprout wings and fly off to the sky like an eagle. (NIV)*

June 19

GIVE THANKS IN EVERY SITUATION

There is always something to be thankful for. You just have to look around for it. In the Bible it says to start the day with a thankful attitude and end the day with it. Give thanks in every situation and in giving thanks to God don't forget from where our blessings come.

You can't look to people who give you presents or money. All the things you get come from God and God alone. You owe thanks only to the Father.

Psalms 103:2 *Praise the Lord, O my soul, and forget not all His benefits.* (NIV)

June 20

YESTERDAY AND TOMORROW

There are only two days in the year that you can do nothing about. One is called yesterday, and the other is called tomorrow; So today is the right day to love, believe, do, and most of all live.

You cannot do anything to change the past or pave the future. It has already been written by God. The only thing you can do anything about is the now---the present.

Many people are worried and anxious about events that will never actually happen to them, so relax and focus on today.

Proverbs 27:1 *Do not boast about tomorrow for you do not know what a day may bring. (NIV)*

June 21

SHAKE IT OFF

Every once in a while, you have to make yourself stop worrying---stop thinking---and just let go. Shake it off and have some fun in your life. Trust me, it'll be worth it.

Over the span of your lifetime, worry can add up to hours and hours of valuable time that you will never get back. Worry is a futile thing. It is like a rocking chair. It will keep you occupied and wont get you anywhere.

Proverbs 12:25 *Anxiety weighs down the heart, but an encouraging word cheers it up. (NIV)*

June 22

STOP COMPLAINING!

As you take a breath right now, another person takes their last breath. Stop complaining and learn to live your life to the fullest with whatever you have.

We all have fallen prey to complaining. Complaining can be summed up in 4 words: "Its all about me."

Complaining is the opposite of thanksgiving. God expects us to be thankful and content in all things.

Take the focus off yourself and thank God for all He has given you.

James 5:9 *Do not grumble against one another, brothers and sisters or you will be judged. The Judge is standing at the door." (NIV)*

June 23

BEING HAPPY IS A CHOICE

Happiness is a choice, not a result. Nothing will make you happy, until you choose to be happy. Nobody will make you happy, unless you decide to be happy. Your happiness will not come to you—it can only come from you.

Have you ever wondered how to be happy? It is a gift from God. True happiness is only found in Jesus Christ. Nothing gives you an everlasting joy and happiness like Jesus.

John 16:33 *I have told you these things, so that in me you may have peace. In this world you will have trouble. But take heart! I have overcome the world! (NIV)*

June 24

TRUE FRIENDS

True friends are those rare people who come to find you in dark places and lead you back into the light. Humans were created to be social creatures and have friends, but be careful of who you let in your world.

Friendship is an important element in a fulfilled, contended life and those who have close friends--- whether one, two, or a multitude, will usually be happy.

Friends can console us when we are in trouble as when Barzillai the Gilleadite consoled David when he was being hunted by Absolam.

But your friends should be chosen carefully because as Paul told the Corinthians, "Bad company corrupts good character." So take caution in how you choose your friends.

Proverbs 12:26 *One who is righteous is a guide to his neighbor, but the way of the wicked leads them astray. (ESV)*

June 25

ONLY GOD SITS HIGH UP

Never look down on anybody. Only God sits that high! Christians should not belittle or judge others. This is not what God teaches us.

Don't be stuck up and think you're better than anyone else. Don't be merciless, greedy and cruel as wolves tearing into the poor, feasting on them.

How an eagle flies high in the sky, how a snake glides over a rock, how a ship navigates the ocean, is all because of God. He is the only one who can judge, condemn, and point fingers. If you condemn others, you will be judged and condemned by God.

Matthew 7:1-5 *Judge not, that ye be not judged. (KJV)*

June 26

ACCEPTING RESPONSIBILITY

The moment you accept responsibility for everything in your life is the moment you gain the power to change anything in your life.

The Bible teaches the concept of personal responsibility saying, "The one who sins, is the one who dies." Personal responsibility is closely related to the law of 'sowing and reaping.'

Each one of us has the personal responsibility to "repent and believe the good news" *(Mark 1:15 "The time is fulfilled and the kingdom of God is at hand. Repent, and believe in the gospel. KJV)*

Romans 1:20 *For since the creation of the world God's invisible attributes, namely his eternal power and divine nature, have been clearly perceived, ever since the creation of the world, in the things that have been made. (NIV)*

June 27

LIFE IS A SERIES OF TINY MIRACLES

Life is a series of tiny little miracles. Take time to notice them. Look at the ladybug that's landed on your hand. Look at the hummingbird whose wings are flapping quicker than the eye can see, and look at the flowers growing wild on the side of a highway.

These are miracles that all come from God. He has created them for you to enjoy, so do not take these things for granted. As the saying goes, 'Take time to smell the roses, for if they are not tended too, even roses die.'

Deuteronomy10: 21 *He is the one you praise; he is your God, who performed for you those great awesome wonders you saw with your own eyes. (NIV)*

June 28

BE IN SOMEONES PRAYERS

The most wonderful places to be in the world are in someone's heart, thoughts, and in someone's prayers.

Prayer is not a mysterious practice reserved only for clergy and the religiously devout. Prayer is simple communicating with God, and for someone to put you in his prayers is a great honor and gift. Being in someone's prayers is the purest form of real love.

To be in someone's hearts is also a blessing, and so is being in their thoughts. Be kind to others and treat them as you would want to be treated.

Philippians 4:6 *Do not be anxious about anything, but in everything by prayer and supplication with thanksgiving, let your requests be made known to God. (ESV)*

June 29

LET GO AND LET GOD

Accept what is---let go of what was--- and have faith in what will be. In Hebrews 11:1 it tells us that faith is "*being sure of what we hope for and certain of what we do not see.*"

Faith is not something we conjure up on our own, nor is it something we are born with; nor is faith a result of diligence in study or pursuit of the spiritual.

When you hold onto something you cannot change, it will bring you down, so you must let it go. Remember, "Let Go and Let God."

Philippians 3:13 *Brothers, I do not consider that I have made it my own. But one thing I do: Forgetting what lies behind and straining forward to what lies ahead. (ESV)*

June 30

NEVER BE A PRISONER OF YOUR PAST

Never be a prisoner of your past. It is just a lesson—not a sentence. Become the architect of your future.

You will never be the same. Life goes on. Remember when one door closes another will open. But you have to be willing to let go of the doorknob. Your past need not be your future. God has a bright future in store for you if you will accept and believe it.

Jeremiah 29:11 *I know the plans that I have for you, declares the Lord. They are plans for peace and not disaster, plans to give you a future filled with hope. (NLT)*

JULY

July 1

REGRETS

Making a big life change is scary. But you know what's even scarier? REGRET. Regret is the worst thing you can have. Change should not be scary if that change is for the better. We may struggle at first, but in the end when you begin to see the results you can smile and say, "I made it!"

Nothing in life is permanent. From childhood to old age or the weather----you must open your mind and accept everything and realize that it's all part of life and a cycle.

Luke 22:32 *But I have prayed for you that your faith may not fail. And when you have turned again, strengthen your brothers. (NASB)*

July 2

GO 'ALL IN'

There is a rare breed of people who go 'all in.' They keep their word and give it their all. They put themselves last for those they care about.

These individuals rarely receive the same compassion and effort, yet continue to give freely. To the givers, forgivers, and selfless lovers out there—Keep pushing forward and don't let this cold world change you.

The world needs to change and you can be the start.

Philippians 2:4 *Let each of you look not only to his own interests, but also to the interests of others. (ESV)*

July 3

SEE THE BRIGHT SIDE OF LIFE

Keep your face always toward the sunshine and the shadows will fall behind you. Positivity is choosing to see the bright side of life. It is recognizing that struggle and pain are not all that's there, even if they are all we can see in that moment.

It's about choosing to see the good in life—believing in the power of encouragement and having hope that things will get better.

A pessimist sees the difficulty in every opportunity—but an optimist sees the opportunity in every difficulty.

Luke 6:37 *Moreover, stop judging and you will by no means be judged and stop condemning and you will be by no means condemned. (NWT)*

July 4

SING LIKE A BIRD

A Chinese proverb says, "A bird does not sing because it has an answer---it sings because it has a song."

Encouraging others and praising them, flows from the heart. It is an involuntary action that comes from recognizing who God is and all He has done and is still doing in your life. It can be as simple as a sunset that reminds us of the love our Father has for us.

Like the bird who sings—your song of praise to God is thanking Him for all He has done.

Psalm 28:7 *The Lord is my strength and my shield—my heart trusts in him and he helps me. (NIV)*

July 5

PAY ATTENTION TO WHAT GOD IS TELLING YOU

Many of us like to make plans. We plan for a vacation next year, or plan for the future. But God sits up there and smiles, saying, "Let them plan, for I'm in control."

Others live 'in the moment' and don't think at all about the future. Once in awhile God will give us a direction about something to prepare for the future, so it is wise to pay attention and listen.

In the Bible if Noah would have ignored God's instruction to build the ark, he and his loved ones would have drowned, too, wiping mankind out completely.

Pay attention to what God is telling you. These "Whispers from God' may seem unlikely to happen at the time, but you have no idea what He has planned and how He wants to use you to make it happen.

Psalm 33:11 *The plans of the Lord stand firm forever—the purposes of His heart through all generations. (NIV)*

July 6

CHANGE YOUR ATTITUDE

Are you discouraged and unhappy with the way your life is going? Do you hate your job and are unhappy with your relationship?

Do you feel unappreciated and that nobody cares about you?

Well, the first step to change the situation is to change your attitude.

The only thing you can change is your attitude towards what's happening. You can start by realizing how much God loves and appreciates you. After all, He made you just the way He wanted. And as you know--- He makes no mistakes.

Ephesians 2:10 *We are Gods handiwork, created in Christ Jesus to do good works, which God prepared in advance for us to do. (NIV)*

July 7

NOTHING CAN SEPARATE YOU FROM JESUS

Nothing can separate you from My love. Let this assurance resonate in your mind, down into your heart and soul. When you start to feel anxious repeat, "Nothing and nobody can separate me from your love, Jesus."

Most people at one time in their life feel unloved and unworthy. They feel alone and abandoned, but be assured that I will NEVER leave you! I will watch over you continually until the end of time.

Others may come into your life, only to disappoint you. I will never turn my back against you, my child.

Romans 8:38-39 *I am convinced that neither death nor life, neither angels nor demons, neither the present not the future, no any powers, neither height or depth, nor anything else in creation will be able to separate us from the love of God that is in Christ Jesus, our Lord. (NIV)*

July 8

IN THIS WORLD YOU WILL HAVE TROUBLE

Give up the idea that you will have a stress-free life. As I told my disciples, *"In the world you will have trouble"*. Do not try to solve your problems by stressing and worrying. Put your energy into the promise I give you of a problem–free life in Heaven.

It is impossible to enjoy me if all you do is worry. My light shines brightly through those who believe and trust in Me.

That kind of trust is supernatural, so when things don't go the way you want them to, put all your trust in Me and I will make it right.

John 16:33 *I have told you these things so that in me you may have peace. In this world you will have trouble, but take heart! I have overcome the world.* (NIV)

July 9

YOU REAP WHAT YOU SOW

You Reap What You Sow. You have heard this saying many times, but may not know how true this really is.

If a farmer plants bad seed, either the outcome will be he will not get any crop, or the crop will be unhealthy and not live long.

If a farmer sows healthy seed it will grow into a nourishing and healthy food.

Part of Adam's curse was that the ground would bring forth thorns and thistle in response to his work, and that "by the sweat of your brow you will eat your food." Adam understood the concept of "you reap what you sow" both literally and figuratively.

Like our first father, Adam, whatever we reap in our life we will sow. In other words, everything you do has repercussions—it comes back to you one way or another. You cannot escape the consequences of your actions. We sow in one season and reap in another. Be careful of your actions for whomever sows generously will also reap generously and whoever sows sparingly will also reap sparingly.

Galatians 6:8 *For the one who sows to his own flesh will from the flesh reap corruption, but the one who sows the Spirit will from the Spirit reap eternal life. (ESV)*

July 10

APPRECIATE WHAT REALLY MATTERS

Slow down and appreciate what really matters. We live in a busy, complicated world and don't take the time to appreciate the things that really matter. Unfortunately, while most people are put on hold while dealing with nonstop demands, they also put Me on hold. The longer you push me into the background, the harder it will be to find Me.

I have called you to follow Me, making your time with Me your # 1 priority. Along the way there will be obstacles for the enemy constantly tries to keep you away from Me, but stay strong and know I am there by your side. As you walk close to Me, I will bless others through you.

John 16:33 *I have said these things to you, that in me you may have peace. In the world you will have tribulation. But take heart: I have overcome the world. (ESV)*

July 11

WHEN LIFE GIVES YOU PROBLEMS—READ THE BIBLE

Life gives us troubles, heartaches, and disappointments. Nobody will have a life stress-free. Everyone finds different ways to cope. Some find temporary relief through alcohol, others with drugs. These are just temporary solutions, like a bandage on a wound. Once the high wears off, the problem is still there.

I personally discovered something that gets me through these turmoil times---reading the Bible. Open the book to a page and see what He is telling you. You might be surprised that whatever page you open is a message just for you.

Remember.... When life gives you more than you can stand...Kneel. (And pray)

Mark 11:24 *So I tell you, whatever you ask for in prayer, believe that you have received it and it will be yours. (NIV)*

July 12

STOP COMPLAINING!

Cultivating a Godly perspective of our spiritual state does not happen naturally. To fight against God's grace and kindness towards us, stop complaining about what you don't have, and thank Him for what you do have!

An attitude of thankfulness should dominate the life of a believer. The enemy, Satan, whispers in our ears to remind us what God has taken away from us.

When this happens, say, "I rebuke you Satan in the name of Jesus Christ," and look at all the things God has given you. You have so much to be thankful for!

1 John 4:4 *You are of God, little children and have overcome them, because he who is in you is greater than he who is in the world. (NKJV)*

July 13

QUENCH YOUR THIRST WITH PRAYER

We know that God is loving, all-powerful, and has the power to heal and take away our suffering. We know God loves us. Still we suffer and wonder why he allows us to endure pain. Doesn't he care? Has he forgotten about us?

We were created to know God and trust in Him, so when our suffering reaches intensity that seems senseless, our only hope is to cling to God in faith.

Like a newborn infant longing for spiritual milk, by drinking it you will have salvation. Your relationship with the Father through His word and prayer is like a baby drinking milk. It fills you up, satisfies you and develops that bond only a baby and his mother can experience.

1 Peter 2:2 *Like newborn infants, long for the pure spiritual milk, that by it you may grow up into salvation. (NIV)*

◆ July 14 ◆

PRAYER IS THE ANSWER

I am a God of overflowing abundance. When you trust Me with your problems and intricate details of your life, you will be pleasantly surprised how I answer your petitions.

When you talk to me in prayer, your faith strengthens as you see how precisely I answer, for I take great pleasure in hearing your requests.

Praying will transform and bless you. Prayer is not a mysterious practice reserved only for the religiously devout. Prayer is simply communicating with God---listening and talking to him.

Come to Me in joyful expectation of receiving what I give to you, for it is My delight in showering you with blessings.

Psalm 37:4-6 *Delight yourself in the Lord, and he will give you the desires of your heart. Commit your way to the Lord; trust in him and he will act. He will bring forth your righteousness as the light and your justice as the noonday. (ESV)*

July 15

NO ONE IS PERFECT

We live in a fallen world—a world tainted by sin. Most of us seek perfection and from this impossible need the result is failure. There is no one or nothing in this world that is perfect.

Sadly, most people seek this fulfillment through other people and things, thus creating idols. Remember---there will be NO other idols besides ME. I am the only one who can fulfill your yearning for perfection.

Exodus 20:3 *You shall have no other gods before me. (NIV)*

◆ July 16 ◆

THE ASSURANCE OF SALVATION

There are many pandemic diseases in the world today. Diabetes, cancer, and multiple sclerosis are just a few that strike people down every day.

Many ask why God allows such diseases to attack people, even those that are believers and live their life for Him. It is hard to imagine our loving God displaying such wrath and anger toward His people, but God's punishments always have the goal of repentance and restoration.

For those who do not know Jesus as Savior, disease is a reminder that life on this earth is tenuous and can be lost at any minute. But because of the blood shed by Christ on the cross, we have the assurance of salvation and the hope of eternity.

Jeremiah 33:6 *Behold, I will bring it health and cure and I will cure them, and will reveal unto them the abundance of peace and truth. (KJV)*

July 17

WISHING FOR A POVERTY FREE WORLD

Why do some people live comfortably while others struggle and starve? In the Bible, God speaks often of the poor and needy. He commands us to give generously to those who are not as fortunate.

Poverty, like disease, is a product of the Fall. It will always be a part of the world as long as the world exists.

Many people believe that happiness and fulfillment are achieved through material prosperity and that real success depends largely on how much a person has.

The Bible teaches that real happiness depends on one's spiritual well being and relationship with God, while human relief efforts have been unsuccessful in bringing the problem of poverty under control.

It says our creator will replace human governments that are driven by self-interest and will compassionately address the needs of the poor. The earth will be a true paradise with housing and food for all, without a trace of poverty.

Reflecting on God's promise of a poverty-free world, reassures those living under oppressive conditions that God cares about them and that the end of their struggles is in sight.

Psalm 72: 12-14 *For he will rescue the poor who cry for help, also the lowly one and whoever has no helper. He will have pity on the lowly and the poor and the lives of the poor he will save. (KJV)*

July 18

CHOOSE YOUR OWN DESTINY

Many people are afraid to die. They are afraid of the unknown. "What happens when I die?" and "Where will I go," are just a few of the things they worry about.

But in the Bible it tells us to fear not, for what awaits us is something we cannot imagine.

God didn't create us to die—that was not His intention. It is the result of sin by Adam and Eve, and every one of us will face death at sometime. When we die we will also face judgment before God.

From the time we are born to when we die, we are given the chance to choose our own destiny. No one can choose it for us—least of all God.

The body dies, but men's spirits live on in one of 2 states: with God or with the devil. Only a personal relationship with Jesus Christ the Son of God can give us life after death.

Proverbs 14:12 *There is a way that appears to be right, but in the end it leads to death.* (NIV)

July 19

GODLY WOMEN

Godly Christian women have been the backbone of the church for numerous years. Older women should teach younger women the skills needed to have a successful marriage.

Throughout history there have been as many Godly women as there have been men. Sometimes their words haven't been preserved as well, but today we do have access to wise words of many strong Christian women.

Christian women can inspire others---and inspiration is subjective, as different people will find different things to be inspiring.

1 Timothy 2:11 *Let a woman learn quietly with all submissiveness. (ESV)*

July 20

GIVE THANKS IN EVERY SITUATION

There is always something to be thankful for. You just have to look around for it. In the bible, it says "Start the day with a thankful attitude and end the day with it." Give thanks in every situation and give thanks to God for where your blessings come from.

You can't look to people who give you material things, all things you get come from God and God alone. You owe thanks only to your Father

Psalm 1:03-2 *Praise the Lord, Oh my soul, and forget not all His benefits. (NIV)*

July 21

VANITY

In Hollywood, vanity is seen more than in any other place. Many people there see themselves as superior to all others. Those with high paying jobs, such as professional athletes are some of the vainest people.

You can see vanity walking down the street by the way someone acts or talks to others. God is opposed to those who are full of themselves. (James 4:6 *God opposes the proud, but shows favor to the humble. NKJV)*

The Biblical notion of vanity conveys a sense of emptiness and lacking—a life without meaning and connection to God.

Solomon wrote more about vanity than anyone else in the Bible, perhaps because he had so much wisdom, had everything he wanted, and had power. Although he had it all and knew a lot about vanity from experience, He humbled himself. (Actually God did it for him.)

Ecclesiastes 1:2 *Vanity of vanities, says the Preacher, vanity of vanities! All is vanity. (ESV)*

July 22

HE RECEIVES US JUST THE WAY WE ARE

If you believe in the Bible, you can believe this. Jesus was with God before the earth existed; He was born of a Virgin; He lived a perfect sinless life; died on the cross for your redemption, and was raised again after three days.

God wants us to come to Him. "Come as you are" is sometimes misunderstood and misapplied today. God is amazing, gracious, and loving.

He calls us to salvation, even though we don't deserve it. Christ died for us making it possible for us to receive forgiveness. He requires us to confess when we come to him, but he receives us just the way we are—then He begins to change us as we submit to Him in obedience.

Matthew 11:28-30 *Come to me, all who labor and are heavy laden and I will give your rest. Take my yoke upon you and learn from me, for I am gentle and lowly in heart, and you will find rest for your souls. For my yoke is easy and my burden is light. (ESV)*

July 23

DARKNESS

Darkness so black that you can hardly see in front of you is terrifying. You can't see what may be lurking in the shadow. You can't see what's around you.

A tiny beam of light could make all the difference in the world.

This is what it is like for the people who don't know Jesus. He is the light of the world, but they do not know Him. As a Christian, you can bring that lightness into their life for the Holy Spirit lives within you.

The Holy Spirit is the source of all light and through Him you will be the conduit. By being the reflector of light, you have the opportunity to bring special God moments into the lives of others.

John 8:12 *Again Jesus spoke to them saying, "I am the light of the world. Whoever follows me will not walk in darkness, but will have the light of life." (ESV)*

July 24

BE THE BIGGER PERSON

Do you want to be a strong woman? A woman who stands up for herself and stands strong for what she believes. Some people see rigidness as strength—living in a box—not accepting anything that doesn't fit inside their box.

Others are more flexible and willing to bend a little. These are the strong women, for they have opportunities to build a relationship with others who have a different mindset.

You can't share your faith walk with people you don't have relationships with. Be willing to bend a little in order to be strong.

Be the bigger person and don't be afraid to be the one who bends to be strong.

***Isaiah* 33:2** *Lord, be gracious to us; we long for you. Be our strength every morning, our salvation in time of distress.* (NIV)

July 25

TRUSTING GOD…ONE DAY AT A TIME

Trust Me one day at a time. By doing this it keeps you close to Me. It is hard for many people to trust, in fear of getting hurt and disappointed. Once you have been wounded, you tend to put a wall up around you—not letting anyone in. But this is not good for you may never find the person I have created to be with you, if you don't give them a chance.

Trust in Me in all circumstances. Don't let your need to understand it all distract you from My presence. With Me by your side you will get through any circumstance or situation.

There are enough worries in this troubled world. Don't get tangled up in a worry-web.

Psalm 84:12 *Lord Almighty, blessed is the one who trusts in you.* (NIV)

July 26

WALK ON YOUR OWN PATH

Right foot. Left foot. Heel to toe. Put one foot in front of the other. Many people live their lives by following a path that someone else paved before.

If you are bored with walking down the same path, be willing to take a risk and try something new. Follow God off the beaten path and see where He leads you. Be open to the unknown and what life has in store for you. With God by your side, there is no wrong way.

Joshua 1:9 *Have I not commanded you? Be strong and courageous. Do not be afraid; do not be discouraged, for the Lord your God will be with you wherever you go. (NIV)*

July 27

STOP TRYING TO PLEASE OTHERS

Beware of trying to please others all the time. It is impossible to please everyone. When you try to please someone else, it is a sign of idolatry. Your concern to please others dampens your desire to please Me.

Through My eyes you can see yourself as one who is deeply loved. Rest in My arms and you will receive deep peace.

What was Jesus response to people pleasing? (John 2:23-25) Here Jesus is described as not entrusting himself to people because He knows what's in people.

People-pleasing is a huge problem among Christian followers. It ultimately creates an idol of people's approval of them. Train your heart to know that the only one you need to please is our Father in Heaven.

Colossians 3:23 *Whatever you do, work at it with all your heart, as working for the Lord, not for human masters. (NIV)*

July 28

IS YOUR GLASS HALF EMPTY OR HALF FULL?

Are you the type of person who thinks the glass is half full or half empty? If you are the latter you most likely make it hard for others to be around you because nothing is ever good enough, big enough, rich enough, or happy enough.

This type of person worries about every little thing: relationships, job, money issues, struggles and other things that suck the life out of you.

Life is a journey and there will be good times and hard times, but the joy of this journey is knowing that you never have to make it alone---God will be with you every step of the way.

Matthew 6:25-27 *Therefore I tell you, do not be anxious about your life, what you will eat or what you will drink, nor about your body, what you will put on. Is not the life more than food and the body more than clothing? (ESV)*

July 29

THANKFULNESS—THE LANGUAGE OF LOVE

A thankful attitude opens the door to Heaven. Spiritual blessings will come to you through this opening. You cannot yet live in Heaven for it is not your time, but you can experience foretastes of your eternal home.

Thankfulness helps your walk on the upward spiral. It is the language of love that enables you to communicate with Me. In the times of trouble I am your refuge and strength.

Thanksgiving and praise put you in a proper relationship with Me, your Father, opening the way for my riches to flow to you. When you thank Me, My presence will fill you with the joy and peace you seek.

1 *Theassalonians* 5:18 *Give thanks in all circumstances for this is the will of God in Christ Jesus for you. (NIV)*

◆ July 30 ◆

CHANGE IS HARD

Change is hard for all of us—at any age. Change stirs up quite a storm in children and adults. When change hits, we feel that our security has been ripped away. Then we may let the stormy waves of fear overtake us.

We may even try to stop the change from happening, or make it unsuccessful, with sinful actions or sinful inaction.

God does not keep silent or answer us in anger, though His anger would be justified. No matter how things look, God has the whole world in His hands.

Romans 8:28 *And we know that in all things God works for the good of those who love Him, who have been called according to His purpose. (NIV)*

July 31

THE END OF THE WORLD

For centuries people have read the Bible and concluded that the world will come to an end. People in every generation wondered, "Will the world literally end? Why? When? How?"

Your concern should not be when the world will end; instead, your focus should be to seek God to be prepared for the times that are coming.

The Bible says the end will come in two main stages: 1) God will destroy organized false religion, and 2) He will turn His attention to the political rulers themselves.

The Bible also says the end will come when mankind has been sufficiently warned by a global proclamation of God's Kingdom.

Be prepared and do not worry. We don't have to wait for the end of the world; we have to work toward it--- not with fear, but with knowing God who saved us is the one we will spend eternity with one day.

***2 Timothy* 3:1-5** *But mark this: There will be terrible times in the last days. People will be lovers of themselves, lovers of money, boastful, proud, abusive, disobedient to their parents. Have nothing to do with such people.* (NIV)

AUGUST

August 1

RAINBOWS

Rainbows are beautiful. There's something majestic about the arch of brilliant colors streaming cross the sky.

The story of rainbows began after the judgment of God when the entire world was covered in a flood. Every living person and animal died except Noah, his family, and the animals on the ark.

Rainbows are a sign of a covenant between God and the world. The rainbow covenant is just one of the many promises He makes us. Rainbows solidify the witness between God and mankind.

A spectrum of a rainbow displays 100 hues, although the human eye only distinguishes red, yellow and blue.

Every time a rainbow shines in the sky remember it's a witness of His promise.

Ezekiel 1:28 *Like the appearance of a rainbow in the clouds on a rainy day, so was the radiance around him. (NIV)*

August 2

I AM THE RESURRECTION AND THE LIFE

I am the Resurrection and the life. People search for life in the wrong ways: Chasing after fleeting pleasures and accumulating worldly treasures that will one day rust and decay.

I offer abundant life to everyone who comes to Me. Come and take my yoke and I will fill you with my life. I do this and bless you with joy and glory.

I have promised to keep you in perfect peace to the extent that you trust in Me. My peace is such an all-encompassing gift.

Philippians 4:6 *Do not be anxious about anything, but in every situation, by prayer and petition, with thanksgiving, present your requests to God. (NIV)*

August 3

IN TIMES OF TROUBLES

Draw to Me in times of troubles. Before you go to a friend or a family member, come to Me. You will never be in control of your own life. Unfortunately, you'll never have a perfect lifestyle, for the only perfect life is when you will be with Me in Heaven.

Until then, relax and trust in My control of your life's circumstances. I promise never to give you anything that you can't handle, and I'll never leave your side.

Rest assured that I am always doing something good for My children. Be on the lookout for all I have prepared for you.

Romans 8:38 *For I am convinced that neither death nor life, neither angels or demons, neither the present nor the future, nor any powers, nor things present, nor things to come. (NIV)*

August 4

EMBRACE THE SIMPLE THINGS

Be thankful for the little things in life. Jesus thanked God for the simple things, such as a small meal (John 6:2-9), for forgiveness (Col. 1:12), and for every day (Psalm 118:24).

Jesus is a wonderful storyteller. He used parables to help us visualize biblical concepts, such as a mustard seed is small, but it will grow into one of the biggest plants.

We are never to be materialistic and become obsessed with possessions. You will never be happy with anything if you're not content with what you have.

Be happy and give God thanks daily, because He created you for a purpose. Laugh, smile, and enjoy what you have. Learn to cherish the small things and count your blessings daily. Enjoy the little things in life, for one day you'll look back and realize they were really big things.

Luke 16:10 *He that is faithful in what is least is faithful also in much: and he who is unjust in what is least is unjust also in much.* (KJV)

August 5

NO NEED TO WORRY

Sit quietly with Me and don't worry about your future. When something pops up in your mind and you worry about what may never happen—take a breath and pray.

There will be times when you project yourself mentally into the next week, month, or year, and you will begin to worry. This is the enemy trying to steer you away from Me.

What you are seeing is a false image, because I am not included in it with you. But fret not for My presence will be with you at all times.

Say to yourself, "Not today, Satan. Jesus is here with me, now and forever!" Then come to the present where you can enjoy Peace in My presence.

Luke 12:22 *Then Jesus said to his disciples: "Therefore I tell you, do not worry about your life, what you will eat, or about your body, what you will wear." (NIV)*

August 6

THE FATHER OF LIES

Lying is one of the most hurtful and wrong things a person can do. Satan is not called, "the father of lies" for no reason. He indeed is the master deceiver. He lies to us on both sides of the sin.

He is the one who tempts us and then he wants us to feel guilty for being tempted, though we haven't yet sinned. When we do succumb to sin, he doesn't want us to come under the conviction of the Holy Spirit. Finally, if the Spirit's conviction reaches us, Satan quickly condemns us.

The Bible is clear that lying is a sin and displeasing to God. Fibs, bluffs, white lies, and half-truths are all considered lies. A lying tongue is something not only God hates, but is also something that is an abomination to Him.

Colossians 3:9 *Do not lie to each other, since you have taken off your old self with its practices. (NIV)*

August 7

YOU ARE RESPONSIBLE FOR YOUR ACTIONS

You can repent of sin and be forgiven, but you may not always be able to alter the outcome. A bad child can pick up a rock and think it would be fun to break someone's window. As soon as he throws it he thinks, "I'm in trouble. God, I'm sorry."

Will God forgive him? Of course He does. But does God stop the rock in mid air and drop it to the ground? I don't think so.

You will be responsible for anything you do that is not looked upon by God as right and good.

The next time you think about doing something you know is wrong and God won't like it---Stop! Your actions speak louder than your words.

John 16:33 *These things I have spoken unto you, that in me ye might have peace. In the world ye shall have tribulation; but be of good cheer; I have overcome the world. (KJV)*

August 8

TRUST

Trusting is a hard thing to do for many people. Once you get burned and lied to by someone, you tend to never trust him/her again. But if you go around and don't trust anyone, you will have a very lonely, sad life.

The only one we know we can trust 100% is our Father who would never lie to us. When you start to doubt something, pray about it. Trust in God's will—even when the spirit is leading in ways you find completely bizarre.

In the Bible, the word "trust" means "a bold, confident, sure security or action based on that security." Trust is not exactly the same as faith; rather, trusting is what we do because of the faith God has given us.

Deuteronomy 7:9 *Know therefore that the Lord your God is God, the faithful God who keeps covenant and steadfast love with those who love him and keep his commandments. (ESV)*

August 9

GOD'S PERFECT TIMING

"I want it, and I want it NOW!" Most of us have zero patience and want things when we want them--- no matter whom it may hurt.

We have to remember that it is not up to us, but God, when we will receive the things we want. We are not in control of our lives---our Father is. The quicker we learn and accept this, the better off we will be.

God has perfect timing. He's never early and He's never late. It takes patience and a lot of faith, but in the end it's worth it!

Jeremiah 29:11 *For I know the plans I have for you, declares the Lord, plans for welfare and not for evil, to give you a future and a hope. (ESV)*

August 10

EXPECT LESS THAN WHAT YOU THINK YOU DESERVE

People will disappoint you, but if you expect less than what you think you deserve, maybe you will be happy. We are human beings, not perfect, and tend to put our needs and feelings before others---thus, many people get disappointed and hurt.

Don't let people discourage you----Just fluff out your tutu and dance away.

This is a scheme used by Satan for he knows that when we are discouraged we will not be the men or women God wants us to be.

Psalms 42:11 *Why are you cast down, O my soul, and why are you in turmoil within me?* (ESV)

August 11

THE DEATH OF A LOVED ONE

"Death takes the body. God takes the soul. Our mind holds the memories. Our heart keeps the love. Our faith lets us know we will meet again."

I read this the other day, and it hit me hard. It is so true, yet we tend to forget. We all lose loved ones. They say, "It gets easier," but it doesn't. Whether it's a parent, spouse, friend or child, losing someone we love is heart wrenching.

Time doesn't make the pain go away, it just eases it a bit. Our faith is in knowing that one day we will meet that loved one again and never be apart.

Psalm 147: 3 *He heals the brokenhearted and binds up their wounds. (NIV)*

August 12

GRASS IS NOT GREENER ON THE OTHER SIDE

Your apartment may not be a 3-bedroom house (but you are not homeless). Your car may not be a Mercedes (but you are not walking), and that job might not be the best (but you are working.)

Be thankful for what you have! You tend to always think the grass is greener on the other side of the fence, but it's not. My children should be thankful for what they have, for someone always has it worse.

I will take care of you forever, until the end of time. Thank Me for what you have and not what you don't.

Rely on Me for the strength to stop fixing your eyes on greener grass and start fixing your eyes on Me.

Ecclesiastes 5:10-14 *He who loves money will not be satisfied with money, nor he who loves wealth with his income; this also is vanity. (ESV)*

August 13

THE BLAME GAME

People all always pointing fingers at others, blaming them for things they may not be guilty of. They are the first to judge and criticize. These are usually the ones who are guilty themselves.

No one has the right to judge you because no one really knows what you have been through. They might have heard the stories, but they didn't feel what you felt in your heart.

Judging others is sinful. There are two forms of judging; one focuses on the motives, while the other focuses on the actions.

God is the only one who has the right to judge you. The Bible says we should not judge others' motives, because if God was to judge our motives and only save us based on the inner righteousness we have on our own, we would be doomed.

Matthew 7: 3-5 *Why do you see the speck that is in your brother's eyes, but do not notice the plank that is in your own eye? (NKJV)*

August 14

SURROUND YOURSELF WITH POSITIVE PEOPLE

There comes a time in life when you walk away from all the drama and the people who create it. Surround yourself with positive, loving people who make you laugh, forget the bad things, and focus on the good.

Love the people who treat you right, and pray for the ones that don't. Life is too short to be anything but happy. YOU are the only one who can make yourself happy.

You can either be negative and sad, or positive and happy: you have the choice.

Falling down is a part of life----getting back up and dusting yourself off is living.

1 *Thessalonians* 5:16-18 *Rejoice always, pray without ceasing, give thanks in all circumstances; for this is the will of God in Christ Jesus for you. (ESV)*

August 15

A STRONG WOMAN

The strength of a woman is not measured by the impact that all her hardships in life have had on her; but the strength of a woman is measured by the extent of her refusal to allow those hardships to dictate her and who she becomes.

It is a known fact that a woman is stronger than a man as far as it is the woman that gives birth--- a man could not bear to go through the labor pains that women do.

A woman's pain in childbirth is part of the suffering brought into the world through sin. This judgment from God was meant to be one that every childbearing woman would experience.

Yes, women are stronger than men in many ways.

Genesis 3:16 *To the women he said, "I will surely multiply your pain in childbearing; in pain you shall bring forth children. (ESV)*

August 16

BREAKING SOMEONE'S HEART

Three things you should never break:

1) Promises
2) Trust
3) Someone's heart.

Some people love another person more than any song can sing and any phrase can express. You are the first thing on their mind in the morning and the last thing every night. You are their drug of choice.

But you don't feel the same way. You aren't a bad person for not returning their love. You're human. It's a painstaking responsibility to break someone's heart, but human beings are complex.

But God will never break your heart. The ONLY relationship where you'll NEVER have your heart broken is the relationship between you and God.

Proverbs 23: 26 *My son, give me thine heart, and let thine eyes observe my ways. (KJV)*

August 17

ACCEPTING JESUS CHRIST AS YOUR SAVIOR

I am your Savior, your deliverer, and preserver. I delivered you from sin and eternal damnation. I rescued you from the domain of darkness and transferred you to the Kingdom of my beloved son.

Have you accepted me as your personal savior? You have all sinned and committed evil acts, *(Romans 3:10-18)* and as a result of sin, you deserve my punishment, but I am a forgiving God.

No one is saved by the faith of others or forgiven by doing good deeds. The only way to be saved is personally accepting Jesus as your Savior.

If you believe Jesus Christ took the punishment so that through faith in Him you will be forgiven, you will spend eternal life with Me in Heaven.

John 3:16 *For God so loved the world, that He gave his only son, that whoever believed in Him should not perish, but have eternal life. (NIV)*

August 18

WHISPERS FROM GOD

This book is called *Whispers From God*. You ask, "How does God whisper to us?" He does it through:

1. **The grandeur of the world**---by showing us the beauty of the world.
2) **God whispers to us through laughter**. Laughter is the best medicine.
3) **He whispers to us through the love of others.**
4) **Through direct address.**

Some hear God speak to them in a dream, through prayer, or reading the Bible. It is a spiritual awakening when God whispers to you. He can use anything to get your attention and to turn your hearts and minds away from the world to Him.

The next time God whispers to you---LISTEN! He lights the path you walk and will never leave you. He is our Father and will never lead us astray.

Psalm 37: 23-24 *The Lord makes firm the steps of the one who delights in Him—though he may stumble, he will not fall for the Lord upholds him with His hand. (NIV)*

August 19

TURN THE PAGE

Don't close the book when bad things happen in your life; just turn the page and begin a new chapter. Things will occur that will be sad, painful, or questionable. You ask God, "Why do you allow these things to happen?"—Especially to a believer.

God created us because He loves us. He never intended for tragedy and prejudice, wars, and hatred, but Adam and Eve rebelled against their creator and caused the first sin which mankind would pay for until the end of time.

You need to reach out to God during these times and He will bring you peace. Like David did in the Bible, when He was in a dark place emotionally, He praised God. He will make things right.

Romans 8:28 *And we know that all things work together for good to them that love God, to them who are the called according to His purpose. (KJV)*

August 20

HELPING OTHERS

Remember whenever you're in a position to help someone in need, be thankful and do it, because that's God answering someone else's prayers through you.

Helping others is God's prescription for depression. In our fallen world, despair and heaviness is everywhere.

We who are strong have an obligation to bear with the failings of the weak and not to please ourselves. (Roman 15:1 ESV)

Giving does not have to be in the form of cash. Helping others includes the times when you visit the sick, run errands for someone who is unable to, or just offer your umbrella to someone on a rainy day.

2 Corinthians 8:9 *For you know the grace of the Lord Jesus Christ, that though he was rich, yet for your sake he became poor, so that you through his poverty might become rich. (KJV)*

August 21

GOD'S PERFECT TIMING

God has PERFECT timing. He's never early, and He's never late. It takes a little patience and a whole lot of faith, but in the end it's worth the wait.

Waiting on God is something believers do. It's about hoping with expectation and trust, knowing that our Lord is not making us wait just to see how long we can.

Many people have trouble with waiting on things. A passive person hopes something good will happen and he will sit around waiting to see if it does. After awhile, they get frustrated and say, "I've waited and nothing happened. I quit."

The expectant person is hopeful and his heart is full of hope. Suddenly what he was waiting for happens.

So don't give up and stop believing. Stay full of hope knowing that God's power is limitless.

Lamentation 3:25 *The Lord is good unto them that wait for Him, to the soul that seeketh Him. (KJV)*

August 22

THIEVES DON'T BREAK INTO EMPTY HOUSES

You keep asking yourself, "Why can't something good happen to me? No matter what I do, I can't get ahead."

It looks like everything good happens to others, but yet, nothing good happens to you.

You pray and pray but still come up empty. You ask God, "Why won't you help me?"

But remember, God never leaves you. It is not our Father that brings turmoil and pain into your life—it's the enemy!

The enemy wouldn't be attacking you if something very valuable wasn't inside you.

Thieves don't break into empty, abandoned houses. You have a purpose and the deceiver of lies will not stop until he succeeds.

Job suffered in many ways and Satan was allowed to do many horrible things to him, but Job knew God is good and continued to trust Him. In the end he was rewarded beyond any expectations he had.

No matter what you are dealing with, be strong and have faith.

Corinthians 4:16 *So we do not lose heart. Though our outer self is wasting away, our inner self is being renewed day by day. (ESV)*

August 23

GOD'S LOVE NEVER FAILS

I can't brag about my love for God, because I fail Him daily. But I can brag about His love for me, because it never fails.

God is love and He loves us. We know that, but often need reminded.

The reality of God's love surrounds us day by day. God's love is steadfast and unchanging. He shows us that through His son, Jesus Christ and the Holy Spirit.

Many of us doubt His love because of broken relationships we have, but because of Christ dying on the cross for us, we no longer have to work toward being loved for it is given freely for all.

Deuteronomy 7:9 *Know therefore that the Lord your God is good, the faithful God who keeps covenant and steadfast love with those who love him and keep his commandments, to a thousand generations. (ESV)*

August 24

HANGING BY A THREAD

You find yourself hanging on the end of the rope. You just had it and can't take anymore. Everything seems to be getting worse and there is no light at the end of the tunnel. But know that nothing is that bad.

If you reach the end of the rope---dive in deeper. There's a place inside of you that knows that nothing is impossible. With God by your side---anything is possible. What is impossible with man, is possible with God!

Jesus himself said, "With God all things are possible," so isn't this far more than the power of positive thinking and trying to solve the problems by yourself?

Matthew 19:26 *Jesus looked at them and said, "With man this is impossible, but with God all things are possible."* (NIV)

August 25

SOLITUDE

For some people it is impossible to shut down their minds. Thoughts stir into worries. The soul usually knows what to do to heal itself, but the challenge is to silence the mind.

Solitude is one of the most important disciplines for the spiritual life. Solitude is being alone with God. It is a way 'to do nothing.'

Solitude and silence is an opportunity to focus on your intimacy with Jesus—to unhook from your daily responsibilities and the people you interact with.

In solitude we bring our self to the Lord to be with Him.

Silence is a source of great faith. Wise men are not always silent, but they know when to be!

Ecclesiastes 9:17 *The quiet words of the wise are more to be heeded than the shouts of a ruler of fools. (NIV)*

August 26

ALLOW THE DOOR TO CLOSE

If the door closes, quit banging on it! Whatever was behind it obviously wasn't meant for you. Consider the fact that maybe the door closed shut because you were worth so much more than what was waiting on the other side.

We've heard, "*If God closes a door, He will open another.*"

Even in the Bible there were doors closing, such as in The Garden of Eden.

Adam and Eve having broken God's commandment were forced to leave Paradise. The gates were shut and an angel was put there at the gate to guard.

Each of us has experienced disappointment. We feel we are doing what God is calling us to do and then we hit roadblocks. But a closed door does not always mean a locked door.

He may want to redirect us to do something better. We are to trust God during those times and wait and see where He leads us and what new doors may open. He may be just putting a hedge of protection around you for something that is not good.

Revelation 3:8 *I know all the things you do, and I have opened a door for you that no one can close. (NLT)*

August 27

ALL MEN WILL FAIL

One thing man has in common is that we all fail at one time in our lives. There isn't one person who will not fail at something---some perhaps more so than others.

The people who never fail are the ones who never do anything or try anything new.

But the most important thing is how we handle failure. People who are willing to try new things may fail, but they are true champions for they do not let their disappointment deter them from trying again.

The assurance is that if you go to God you will find all the fullness awaiting you there.

1 Corinthians 10:12 *So if you think you are standing firm, be careful that you don't fall.* (NIV)

August 28

FOCUS ON THE GOOD

We all have people in our lives that try to bring us down. It may a parent, boss, or friend that criticizes you.

Sometimes those with low self-esteem will try to bring others down for misery loves company.

There comes a time in life when you have to walk away from all the drama and the people who create it. Surround yourself with people who make you laugh, forget the bad things, and focus on the good.

Love the people who treat you right, and pray for the ones who don't.

Life is way too short to be anything but happy. Falling down is part of life, but getting back up is living.

The Bible says to ignore people that try to bring you down and tels you to always have a positive attitude, which will help you when you are amidst these people.

Don't take offense, take root in your heart and pray for them.

Proverbs 24:16 *For though the righteous fall seven times, they rise again, but the wicked stumble when calamity strikes. (NIV)*

August 29

YOU CAN'T TAKE IT WITH YOU

The way of the world is to work hard and make a lot of money so you can buy nice things. The problem is the more things people get, the more they want. When we don't have what others may have, we feel like a failure.

But what is real abundance? Forget all the earthly possessions you have and what's left in your life is what matters. The #1 thing that really matters is your relationship with God.

Abundance is not the 'stuff' you may have sitting in your garage or what you are wearing---it is having a healthy, loving relationship. Start with God and move down the line.

When you are called home all those pretty things will not be going with you. All the money you accumulated cannot be buried with you.

Colossians 3:2 *Set your minds on things above, not on earthly things. (NIV)*

August 30

SAYING GOODBYE

In your life, one day you will have to lose someone you love. Whether it's a spouse, friend, relative or the unbearable pain of losing your child.

Saying the final goodbye is an emotion that is full of grief and may consume you. You now have to take the next step of going on living without them. It's heart-wrenching.

You may have fear of living alone and don't know who to turn to. First, allow your friends to be with you and help with your grief. Second and the most important thing to remember is you are NEVER alone!

God is always with you. He knows how you feel and the pain you are feeling. He cares more than anybody else about you and will get you through this. Just lean on Him and let Him know you trust and love Him.

Revelation 21:4 *He will wipe away every tear from their eyes, and death shall be no more, neither shall there be mourning, nor crying, nor pain anymore, for the former things have passed away. (ESV)*

August 31

I AM YOUR SHEPHERD

Come to me with all your weaknesses. Rest assured that nothing is impossible with Me.

When anxiety tries to put a wedge between you and Me, remind yourself that I am Omnipotent, Omniscient and Omnipresent. I am not only "high capacity" but I'm "infinite capacity."

I never sleep and am perfect in all abilities. There isn't one single thing that I don't know, and unlike humans who can only be at one place at one time, I am everywhere at the same time.

I am your shepherd and you are my sheep. I will watch over you and protect you from evil and the enemy.

Matthew 10: 29-30 *Are not two sparrows sold for a penny? And not one of them will fall to the ground apart from your Father? But even the hairs on your head are all numbered. (NLT)*

SEPTEMBER

September 1

BE HAPPY IN YOUR OWN SKIN

Most people are not happy in their own skin. They want to change the color of their hair, eyes, and body structure. Today, it is easy to be able to do these things. You can go to a drug store and purchase hair dye to change your hair color; the optometrist sells colored contact lenses and the plastic surgeon can shorten your nose or enlarge your breasts.

But God made you the way He wanted you to look. Each and every one of us are unique and an individual. No two people look alike---even twins.

Learn to love what you look like and appreciate what our Father did when He created you in His image.

Variety is the spice of life. Give thanks to Him and quit putting yourself down. In His eyes you are beautiful! So does it really matter what anyone else thinks?

The Bible says that we need to take a different approach to appearance than fitting into todays' idea of beauty.

Remember---true beauty lies within and never fades or wrinkles.

Matthew 23:28 *Outwardly you look like righteous people, but inwardly your hearts are filled with hypocrisy and lawlessness. (NLT)*

September 2

LIVE LIFE IN JOY

Choose to live life in joy. Life goes by in the blink of an eye. It's too short to live angry, resentful or ungrateful.

If you look for the good in things, and the good in people, you will find it. Choose to be happy and at peace. Decide that each day is going to be great and make each moment count.

Refuse to let negative thoughts root in your mind and negative people bring you down. Try to make your journey in life a positive and good one---don't let obstacles and bumps along the way bring you down.

If you make a mistake---it's okay, for everyone does. See it as a lesson and move forward. Spend less time worrying and more time being grateful for the things you have and the people who love you.

James 4: 14 *Yet you do not know what tomorrow will bring. What is your life? For you are a mist that appears for a little time then vanishes. (ESV)*

September 3

THE DEVIL IS REAL!

The devil is real! He can appear in many forms: A serpent, a wolf dressed in sheep clothing or the grotesque red figure with horns and a tail. But he is real!

Satan is alive and well and he seeks to destroy you. The Apostle Peter says in 1 Peter 5:8 "*Your adversary the devil walks about like a roaring lion, seeking whom he may devour.*" (NIV)

Satan has a scheme, but God has a plan.

The devil hates you because every time he sees you, he sees God. Satan despises you because God loves you so much. The devil doesn't want you to know that God promises you can live free from fear by speaking God's word against the devil.

There are 6 strategies the devil uses. They are stealth, ignorance, unbelief, distraction, doubt, and outright lies.

The war between God and Satan is for your soul, but we walk in obedience to God. Equip yourself for spiritual warfare by reading the Bible and through prayer.

1 John 3:8 *Whoever makes a practice of sinning is of the devil, for the devil has been sinning from the beginning.* (ESV)

September 4

EVERYONE HAS A STORY TO TELL

Everyone has a story to tell about their life—some are more exciting than others. I believe that everyone has a best seller. You are the co-author of your story and the only one who can make it successful. Your attitude, beliefs and with the help of the author, Jesus Christ, it can be nothing but a hit.

Have faith, perseverance and whenever you feel like you are losing a battle, say to yourself, "I don't know how my story will end, only God knows --- but nowhere in my book will it ever read, *'I quit or gave up.'*"

Be a best selling author and make the story of your life a hit.

2 Chronicles 15:7 *But as for you, be strong and do not give up for your work will be awarded. (NIV)*

September 5

TEAMWORK

There is no better teacher than THE HOLY SPIRIT and no better text than GOD'S WORD.

With God by your side, how can you lose? Teamwork is essential to make anything a success. For a team to run smoothly you must work together in an effective manner. Do nothing out of selfish ambition or vain conceit, but the two of you together are better than one.

As a team each person has his own special ability that they can offer. Christ is the captain of our salvation—He controls the vessels speed and direction of our life and through Him we will reach our final destination.

1 Corinthians 3:9 *For we are all God's fellow workers, you are God's field, God's building.* (NIV)

◆ September 6 ◆

ARE YOU SPIRITUALLY DRAINED?

All things—even things affecting me right now are God's servants. The circumstance, people, and events around me are all under God. They are all His servants, designed to help and bless me spiritually.

Next time you feel spiritually drained, remember that you have a choice. You can feel happy or sad. You can wrap yourself in excuses, self-pity, and 'I should-have' or 'I wish I could have'---or you can choose to draw strength from an unchanging and loving God.

God controls and allows every detail in our lives. Nothing happens without His knowledge and approval.

Psalms 31:24 *Be of good courage, and he shall strengthen your heart, all ye that hope in the Lord. (KJV)*

September 7

MISTAKES ARE LESSONS

When we realize we are children of God, our perspective in life changes. Like children, we are constantly developing, growing, and changing.

Along the way we will make mistakes and do the wrong thing. Like a good father, God will never give up on us. He allows us to make mistakes so we can learn from them. We should not be surprised when He disciplines us, for that is His way of correction or improvement.

Our ultimate nature will not be clear until we are present with Him, but until that time we will continue to change. Until we are present with Him, we may question why things are happening, but when we do, we will be like Him.

God is constantly shaping us and helping us to mature and become more like Jesus. Trust Him and obey His word for He is our Father and knows what is right for us.

John 1:12 *But to all who did receive Him, who believed in His name, He gave the right to become children of God. (ESV)*

September 8

SELF LOVE

Everybody today is out to please #1. Instead of looking to help others, they only seek to satisfy their own personal needs.

There are so many people that have less than you do, but you only look at what it is you need and want.

Do nothing out of selfishness or out of vanity and glory: rather, humbly regard others as more important than yourselves.

Scripture warns us about self-love. Our focus should not be on ourselves. Loving yourself too much shows selfishness and arrogance which God hates.

Philippians 2:4 *Let each of you look not only to his own interests, but also to the interest of others. (ESV)*

September 9

SLOW DOWN—DON'T DANCE SO FAST

Have you ever watched children on a Merry-Go-Round? Did you ever follow a butterfly's flight or merely watch the sun fade into the night?

If not, you better slow down and don't dance so fast, because time is short and the music won't last. You are missing life's greatest gifts.

When you're lying in bed at the end of the day and you're mind is in overdrive with all the things you have to do, shut your mind off.

Life isn't a relay race. You better slow down before your song is over.

Thessalonians 5:16 *Be joyful always, pray continually; give thanks in all circumstances, for this is God's will for you in Christ Jesus. (NIV)*

◆ September 10 ◆

MAKE TIME FOR GOD

As you opened your eyes this morning, I hoped you would find time to talk to Me. But I noticed you were too busy figuring what you are going to wear, and running around getting the kids ready for school.

I hoped you would find time for Me…but you didn't.

Then I saw you jump up and I thought you were going to talk to Me, but you ran to the phone to call a friend. You would rather talk to her, than Me.

At bedtime you were exhausted and after you tucked the kids in, you plopped into bed and fell asleep. I so much wanted to talk to you, but again I didn't come first in your busy life.

I love you so much that every day I wait for a thank you or just a word from you. Well….maybe tomorrow. I'll be waiting!

Your friend,
God.

James 5:16 *The prayer of a righteous man is powerful and effective. (NIV)*

◆ September 11 ◆

THE BEAUTY OF A HAND

Did you ever look at a newborn baby's hands? They are delicate and fragile. Take a look at a gardener's hands-- they are weathered from years of gardening.

Hands are amazing for without them we cannot feel, touch or touch someone and make them feel wanted.

But the most amazing hands of all time were Jesus' hands. He performed miracles with them, by laying them on a blind or crippled person.

His hands broke bread and fish to feed thousands. Jesus' hands blessed the sun, warmed heads of children, and opened the skies.

Thank God for simple things like your 2 hands He gave you---just another gift from your loving Father.

Isaiah 49:16 *Behold, I have engraved you on the palms of My hands; your walls are continually before Me. (NIV)*

September 12

I WILL LEAD YOU OUT OF THE VALLEY

Life is not always easy. We will experience times of despair and excruciating pain. These are times when we think we can't go on anymore or endure one more minute of agony. This is our darkest valley.

You are fearful, confused, and don't know where to turn. When you experience these times, do not despair for I am there with you. Even in your darkest moments you have nothing to fear because I will not leave you. Even though you don't see me, say, "I fear no evil; for you are with me."

I am the Shepherd and you are my sheep and I will lead you out of all valleys.

2 Samuel 22:29 *For thou art my lamp, O Lord, and the Lord will lighten my darkness.* (KJV)

September 13

WORRYING IS THE DEVIL'S TRICK

There are those people who are called "worry warts" for they worry about everything. I unfortunately am one of them.

Even the simplest little things or things they cannot do anything to change the outcome.

Worry is the Devil's trick. It can make you sick if you allow it to. It fills your mind with doubt, telling you things will never work out.

Worrying won't help you solve a problem or bring about a solution, so why waste your energy on it?

The Devil loves when you worry because it shows him you don't have enough faith in Me. So the next time you start to worry----pray to Me.

Feed your faith and cast your cares on Me every day. Worried thoughts do nothing but make you distressed, but I am good and want you blessed.

Matthew 6:27-29 *Can all your worries add a single moment to your life? Any why worry about clothing? Look at the lilies of the field and hoe they grow. They don't worry or make their clothing, yet Solomon in all his glory was not dressed as beautiful as they are. (NLT)*

September 14

BE MORE LIKE JOB

We know that God is loving and all-powerful. We know He has the power to heal and take our suffering away. We know He loves us unconditionally, but there are times when we wonder, "Has He forgotten me? Has He turned His back on me?"

You wonder how a God so great and loving can allow you to go through something as painful as what you are experiencing.

During these times, remember Job, and you'll find a Godly man who experienced agony beyond anything we could comprehend.

He was the richest man on earth and when Satan went to God asking to let him take away everything Job had, to see if he would remain faithful to God, He allowed it. Job lost his sheep, his oxen, his camels, his servants and all his children---but he did not lose his faith in God.

In the end we see Job emerges with his faith with God intact.

We need to be like Job when we are tempted and never lose faith in Christ Jesus.

Job 1:8 *The Lord said to Satan, "Have you considered my servant Job? There is no one on earth like him; he is blameless and upright, a man who fears God and shuns evil."* (NIV)

September 15

THE RICHEST OF ALL

You can work hard all of your life to gather riches and wealth. You can buy a big house, fancy car, designer clothes, and a bank account that is the envy of your friends and family.

You can buy a yacht, travel around the world, and attend the parties of 'the rich and famous,' but you cannot take them with you when I call you home.

The only things you can take with you when you leave this world are the things that are packed inside your heart.

Be kind and help one another and set an example to others for that is what I consider the richest of all.

1 *Timothy* 6:10 *For we brought nothing into this world, and it is certain we can carry nothing out. (KJV)*

September 16

LETTING GO

Sometimes it's better to just let things be as they are, let people go who really doesn't want to stay, don't fight for closure, don't ask for explanations and don't expect people to understand where you're coming from.

If you do the right thing, you don't owe anything to anybody.

Letting go is one of the hardest things to do, but we must trust that our Lord has something better for us.

It will be easier to let things go when we realize God is in control of everything. *"Let Go and Let God."*

Jeremiah 29:11 *"For I know the plans I have for you," declares the Lord, "plans for welfare and not evil, to give you hope and a future."* (NIV)

September 17

NOT TODAY, SATAN!

When the devil goes after the ones you love---you fight harder. You pray and love with all you got. He is relentless, knows our weakness, and which strings to pull.

But when he goes after someone close to you, it really becomes personal! Your claws come out and you are ready to fight and win the battle.

The next time the devil attacks you or someone you love, say a prayer to God for his help and say, "NOT TODAY SATAN!"

John 10:10 *The thief comes only to steal and kill and destroy. I came that they may have life and have it abundantly. (NIV)*

September 18

LIVE TODAY AS IF IT WERE YOUR LAST DAY

"Wake up and strengthen the things that remain, which were about to die; for I have not found your deeds completed in the sight of My God. So, remember what you have received and heard and keep it, and repent.

Therefore if you do not wake up, I will come like a thief and you will not know at what hour I will come to you." (Revelation 3:2-3)

We must be prepared for when our time on Earth is up and we are called home to Heaven. Live today as if it were your last day and abide by His rules. When it is your time, you shall have no fear.

Romans 5:12 *Therefore just as sin came into the world through one man, and death through sin, and so death spread to all men because all sinned. (NIV)*

September 19

A PROMISE TO MYSELF

I promise myself that nothing can disturb my peace of mind. To talk health, happiness, and prosperity, to every person I meet.

I promise to think only of the best, to work only for the best, and to expect only the best.

I promise to forget the mistakes of the past and press on to the greater things of the future. I promise to give so much to improving myself, that I will have no time to judge or criticize others.

I promise to think well of myself and to proclaim to the world, not in boastful words, but in great deeds. And I promise to live in the faith of our Father and thank Him for all He has given me.

Psalms 1:1 *Blessed are those who do not walk in step with the wicked, or stand in the way that sinners take, or sit in the company of mockers. (NIV)*

September 20

BE A GOOD EXAMPLE

You are the only Bible many unbelievers will ever read. Be the type of example they may look up to and want to follow. Imitation is the sincerest form of flattery.

We are all impacted by a wide range of different people. Some are good, and others are dangerous and harmful. If you imitate well, others will imitate you---it is a cycle of imitation, reproduction and discipleship.

Are you a person others want to follow? Are you characterized by faith, love and hope? By joy and thanksgiving? By prayer and dependence upon God?

Be the role model you can be proud of and God can shine on.

Matthew 5:16 *Let your light so shine before men, that they may see your good works, and glorify your Father which is in Heaven. (KJV)*

September 21

YOU CANNOT REWIND YOUR LIFE

Do you sometimes wish you could rewind time back to the good ole days and press pause? Just for a little while.

Those carefree, happy days when everything in your life was perfect. Perhaps you would like to go back to when you were a child, living life with your family.

Maybe when you first got married and life was as good as it gets, or when you brought home your first bundle of joy.

But there is no going back. That was the past, and no matter how much you would like to be there again---it will never happen.

Leave the past in the past, no matter how hurtful or happy it may be. No amount of wishing, worry or attempts to bring it back will work.

It may not be easy, but strive to forget what lies behind and live today with the blessed hope of the eternal things ahead.

Isaiah 43: 18-19 *Forget the former things, nor consider the things of old. Behold, I am doing a new thing, now it springs forth, do you not perceive it? I will make a way in the wilderness and rivers in the desert. (ESV)*

September 22

DO YOU LIVE FOR WEALTH OR FOR THE GLORY OF GOD?

No matter how good or bad your life is, wake up each morning and be thankful that you still have one.

Before you get out of bed, thank Me for the blessings I have given to you: The roof over your head—the food in the refrigerator, and the car in your driveway.

Instead of wishing for a better car, bigger house, or steak and lobster on the table instead of hamburger meat---give thanks for what you do have.

Chances are you have more than 80% of the people in the world.

Everyone likes material things. That is not a sin. When the need for possessions becomes obsessive you are in idolatry and need to repent. Ask yourself, "Do you live for your wealth, or for the glory of God?"

1 John3: 17 But if anyone has the world's goods and sees his brother in need, yet closes his heart against him, how does God's love abide in him? (ESV)

September 23

WORDS OF WISDOM

Never give up and never lose hope. Always have faith for it allows you to cope. Trying times will pass as they always do.

Have patience and your dreams will eventually come true. So for today, put on a smile and live through the pain knowing "This too shall pass" and from it the strength you will gain.

God will help you through your trials and these trials will make you stronger.

Don't take my word for it—believe in His promises. When things are going bad, that's when you will glorify God and trust in Him because you know He can only help you.

Pray continuously. Sometimes God may not answer right away-- in our way or our time--- but He answers in the best way at the best time!

2 Chronicles 15:7 *But as for you, be strong and do not give up, for your work will be rewarded. (NIV)*

September 24

WHEN THINGS GO WRONG

When things don't go exactly as you would like them to-- learn to accept the situation. If you start to worry and fret, these feelings can easily spill over into resentment. Once you realize that I am in control—not you--- you will be able to accept it and move on.

One of the most important keys that will make it possible for us to walk in kingdom living is our expression of praise. We are to bless God at all times, not just when things go smoothly. We are to bless Him when things go wrong, too. Thank Him for the good and thank Him for the bad.

1 Peter 3:8 *Finally, all of you, be like-minded, be sympathetic, love one another, be compassionate and humble. (NIV)*

September 25

WORRYING IS LIKE SITTING IN A ROCKING CHAIR

Worry is a senseless emotion for there is nothing you can do about most of the things you worry about. Chances are that 90% of the things you worry about will never happen. All worrying does is cause you sleepless nights, ulcers, gray hairs and anxiety. Who wants any of those things?

Worrying is like sitting in a rocking chair. It will give you something to do, but you will never get anywhere!

Worrying is the opposite of trust. When you worry it shows God you don't believe in Him for He says, "Which of you by worrying can add one cubit to his stature?"

When you turn your worry into worship, God will turn your battles into blessings.

Matthew 6:30 *And if God cares so wonderfully for wildflowers that are here today and thrown into the fire tomorrow, he will certainly care for you. Why do you have so little faith? (NLT)*

◆ September 26 ◆

LIFE IS WHAT YOU MAKE IT

Life is only what you make it. Fall in love and dream BIG. Laugh everyday, and tell stories. Reminisce about the good old days, but look with optimism to what the future holds.

Learn more and be creative. Spend time with people you love, and love with all your heart. Never, ever, give up and do what you love.

Be true to who you are and make time for the 'simple' things in life. Forgive, even when it's hard to do, and be the change you wish to see in this crazy world.

Try new things and work hard. Embrace yourself and trust in yourself. Be thankful for EVERYTHING and be nice to EVERYONE.

Live for today, but most of all, make every moment count. And last but not least, give thanks ALWAYS to God for everything He has done for you.

1 Theassalonians 5:18 *In everything give thanks, for this is the will of God in Christ Jesus concerning you. (NKJV)*

September 27

RIDING ON THE TRAIN OF LIFE

Life is like riding on a train—The train of life. It begins when we first board—the day we are born. That's the day we are introduced to our parents on earth.

As you grow, other people will board. Some will be significant (siblings, friends, your children, and your soul mate) while others, not so much (mere acquaintances).

This is when your parents will step down off the train, letting you take the journey without them. It may be scary at times, but it is necessary.

Others will also step off from time to time. But one person who will NEVER step off is your Lord, Jesus Christ.

Through all the ups and downs and bumps along the journey, He will be there protecting you until you reach your final destination—Eternal life with Him in Heaven.

Enjoy the ride!

Hebrews 13:5 *Keep your lives free from the love of money, and be content with what you have, for God has said, "I will never leave you, nor forsake you."* (NKJV)

◆ September 28 ◆

SPREAD YOUR WINGS AND FLY!

When you do the very best you can, you never know what miracle is wrought in your life, or in the life of another.

When you find yourself in a situation that you think is impossible to get through… take a breath…then step forward…spread your wings and fly!

2 Peter 5:7-8 *Casting all your care on Him, because He cares about you. (KJV)*

September 29

THROUGH THE BUMPS, THE RIDE GOES ON

On the ride called life you have to take the good with the bad. You make yourself smile, even when you are sad. You love what you do have, and remember (with joy) what you once had. You learn to always forgive, but never forget.

Along the journey you learn from all your mistakes, but learn never to regret. People in your life change—and sometimes, not for the better. Things will go wrong—no matter how hard you try for them not to, but through all these bumps along the ride, remember---The ride will go on!

Make the trip of your life a good and humble one. Never take things for granted and always give God thanks.

James 1:2-3 *Count it all joy, my brothers, when you meet trials of various kinds, for you know that the testing of your faith produces steadfastness. (ESV)*

September 30

A TEA BAG

The longer the tea bag sits in the cup, the stronger the tea. The more God's Word saturates our minds, the clearer it is we understand what's important to Him.

How does God expect us to view and use His word—the Bible? Almighty God demanded Moses to read His word.

He says He esteems the person, "who trembles at my word," and Jesus Christ said that, "Man shall not live by bread alone, but by every word that proceeds from the mouth of God."

There are 3 things we must believe about God's word. They are:

1) God's word is true.
2) God's word demands what is right
3) It provides what is good.

Like the tea bag that grows stronger as it sits in the cup, your faith will grow stronger as you read The Bible.

Psalm 119:75 *I know, Oh Lord, that your rules are righteous.* (ESV)

OCTOBER

October 1

LEARN TO TALK

A lot of problems in the world would disappear if we only took the time to talk to each other, instead of talking about each other. Gossip is detrimental in a relationship. It's in poor taste to denigrate someone behind his back. Whether its spreading rumors, speaking critically, or badmouthing someone, it's a bad idea and something God doesn't tolerate.

Life has enough problems. We don't really know what someone is going through. If you have to talk about someone, talk positively. The Bible tells us "We reap what we sow." With that in mind, gossip is a way to make the listener question something about the character of a person.

When you are about to say something about someone, stop and ask yourself, "Could it hurt that person?" If so, bite your tongue.

Proverbs 16:28 *A perverse man stirs up dissention, and a gossip separates close friends.* (NIV)

October 2

THE ROCK

Did you ever go to a river or lake and notice a rock lying near the edge of the rapids? Clinging to the rock is a small fragile tree. Turbulent waters swept past the tree as it held on tightly. It seemed like the current would engulf it and wash it away. But the rock was determined to keep it safe.

Jesus is our rock. We can cling to Him in troubled times, but He will never get overtaken by the raging waters. He provides us with a firm foundation against any situations life throw at us.

He will soothe our hearts and calm us. The safest place to be in a storm is with our roots sunk deeply into the rock of our salvation. Hold on tight to Jesus.

Psalm 63:8 *My soul clings to you, Your right hand upholds me. (ESV)*

October 3

SPIRITUAL MILK

Like newborn infants, we long for spiritual milk. By drinking it, we grow with salvation. Our relationship with the Father and our thirst for His daily bread through His word and prayer should be like that of a child drinking His mother's milk.

Are you well fed? Do you fill your minds, bodies, and spirits full of daily bread? Or do your actions show that you are actually starving because you are not feeding from His word?

Do you enjoy the actual words God has written: His life story, blessings, sovereignty, and loving kindness? The only way to be satisfied and healthy is by opening the Bible and refrain from the evils of the world. If you keep drinking the milk (reading the Bible) you will flourish. If you quit, it will curdle and sour.

John 4:14 *But whoever drinks the water that I will give them will never be thirsty again. The water that I will give them will become in them a spring of water welling up to eternal life. (ESV)*

October 4

RISE UP AND DUST YOURSELF OFF

You are walking down the street, stumble, and fall over a random object on the sidewalk. You scrape your knee. The person walking behind you saw you fall and laughs.

So it is on your walk through life with the Lord. Satan would love nothing more than for you to fall and dwell in your humiliation, but the Lord wants you to rise up, dust the dirt off your clothes, and move forward. You may stumble on this long journey called life, but do not fear for Jesus is holding you up with His right hand.

He is faithful and will never forsake or abandon you. He knows what you need and what you're going through. He knows your pain. Commit to Him and live by His word, knowing that in all situations He will help you.

1 Proverbs 24:16 *For though the righteous fall seven times, they rise again, but the wicket stumble when calamity strikes.* (NIV)

October 5

CAREFULLY CHOOSE YOR FRIENDS

The best people are the ones that come into your life and make you see the sun on a cloudy day. They're the kind of people who believe in you so much that you start believing in yourself.

They're the type of person who loves you unconditionally--- simply because you are you, and you don't try to be someone else.

When you find this type of person hang on to them tightly for time is precious. Make sure you spend it with the right people. It is important that Christians carefully choose their friends.

Just like a good parent tries to remove negative influences from their child's life, God will remove bad influences from our life and replace them with Godly friends.

So if someone who you thought was a friend and they suddenly avoid you---it is God taking them away for He knows who is good for you and who isn't.

Proverbs 23:20 *Do not carouse with drunkards or feast with gluttons, for they are on their way to poverty and too much sleep clothes them in rags. (NLT)*

October 6

RELATIONSHIPS

Relationships! One of the hardest things you will go through in your life. You may be one of those people who go through one relationship after another, but still have no luck.

But remember that there is no relationship that is a waste of time. If it didn't bring you what you want, it taught you what you didn't want.

Do not allow your loneliness to lower your standards. Don't look for someone who will fix everything for you: look for someone who will stay by your side while you fix yourself, while motivating you.

Man was created not to be alone but to grow old and love another person. Don't settle. Wait until God sends you the right person. He is a much better judge of character than you are.

Romans 8:29 *For those God foreknew, he also predestined to be conformed to the image of his Son, in order that he might be the firstborn among many brothers. (NIV)*

October 7

A POEM ON LOSING A LOVED ONE

You never said you were leaving,
You never said goodbye.
You were gone before I knew it,
And only God knows why.

In life I loved you dearly,
In death I love you still.
In my heart you hold a place,
That no one could ever fill.

Death is not a finality like many people think. The Bible tells us that everyone is affected by 'The Fall of Adam and Eve'; thus we all must die.

The minute one becomes a follower of Jesus they are God's children. Death will come to everyone, but for the believer, death is the beginning of a wonderful new existence with God.

Romans 8:1 *There is therefore now no condemnation for those who are in Christ Jesus, who walk not after the flesh, but after the Spirit. (KJV)*

October 8

LIVE IN THE PRESENT

Don't cry over the past, for it's gone.
Don't stress about the future, because it hasn't arrived yet.
Learn to live in the present and make every second count.
Today is truly a present from God, for everything from here on hinges on this.

The Bible teaches us about time management.
Our earthly sojourn is significantly shorter than we think.
Seek to change your use of time by first reflecting.
Make a concerted effort to consider your time management and enjoy every day as if it was your last.

Matthew 6:19-21 *Do not store up for yourselves treasures on earth, where moth and rust destroy and where thieves break in and steal. But store up for yourselves treasures in heaven, where neither moth nor rust destroys and where thieves do no break in and steal. (BSB)*

October 9

NEVER GIVE UP

Turn your worry into worship and sit back and watch God turn your battles into blessings.

When you are preoccupied by problems, you have an option. Shift your focus to something positive.

Satan's target is your mind and his weapon is lies. Fill your mind with God's word and He will win the battle against the devil.

God is saying to you today---The pain will end, the tears will stop, and I will open doors to a season of miracles and blessings. Never give up!

Gallatians 6:9 *And let us not grow weary of doing good, for in due season we will reap, if we do not give up. (NIV)*

October 10

THE DEVIL IS A LIAR!

The devil wants you to worry about your future so you won't be able to enjoy your life right now. But remember he is a liar! Enjoy every minute of your life because it is a gift from your Father.

Never once does the Bible say, "Worry about it—stress over it or figure it out." It reads over and over, "Trust in God."

Whenever you do not understand what's happening in your life, just close your eyes, take a deep breath and say, "God I know it's your plan. I trust in you. Just help me through it."

Corinthians 2:9 *Eye has not seen nor ear heard, nor have entered into the heart of man the things of which God has prepared for those who love Him. (NKJV)*

October 11

HAVE PATIENCE: GOD IS WORKING ON IT!

Today as you open your eyes, your mind starts thinking about the problems you have in your life. You're in bed wondering how to solve a situation that seems out of your hands, but fear not for God says, "Be still and know I'm already at work."

Have patience and wait on God's timing and you'll have a better result than if you try to solve it alone. Rushing things will do no good. Pray for patience and understanding and sit back and watch God work it out.

Psalm 9:10 *Those who know your name trust in you, for you Lord, have never forsaken those who seek you. (NIV)*

October 12

LEARN TO APPRECIATE A SIMPLE LIFE

There is no condemnation for those who love Me. I died for you so you may be free. The journey you will take in this world will have troubles and problems. You must keep your focus on Me.

If you stray and follow the way of the world with all its glamour and fancy material things, you will start to descend into a black hole---one you may not be able to get out of.

Troubles are tools by which I allow you to encounter to give you better things.

Learn to live and appreciate a simple life. By doing this, you will feel the peace I offer.

Psalm 46:1 *God is our refuge and strength, an ever-present help in trouble.* (*NASB*)

October 13

BE DIFFERENT

Don't be like everyone else—be different. Do the work others aren't willing to do and you will get the things others will never have.

Be willing to step outside the box and try something new and exciting. Stop doing the things you have been doing on autopilot.

Insanity is doing the same thing over and over again and expecting different results. Be a leader and not a follower in life.

Psalm 139: 13-14 *You alone created my inner being. You knitted me together inside my mother. I will give thanks to you because I have been so amazingly and miraculously made. Your works are miraculous, and my soul is fully aware of this.*

October 14

WE WILL ALWAYS BE GOD'S CHILDREN

Being an adult is a big responsibility. Some of us are single parents taking on double duty both in finances and rearing our children.

We have to do our work, take care of our homes, and deal with problems that pop up unexpectedly.

Being a grown up doesn't have to mean we can't enjoy ourselves and have a little fun in life. We sometimes wish we were children again, for when we were young we had no problems or cares for our parents took care of them.

Joy should be more a part of life even for adults, because in God, our Father's eyes, we still are children ---HIS.

He created a wonderful, beautiful world for us to live in---even if we are dealt problems at times.

Let your hair down and don't take things so seriously. Have some fun, thank God for all He's given you, and worship with joy.

Exodus 23:12 *Work six days, rest on the seventh.* (MEV)

October 15

COMPLAINING IS NOT A FRUIT OF THE SPIRIT

"I want that--- why can't I have it?" "I'm too fat, how come she can lose weight and I have a hard time?" "Why does her baby sleep all night and mine is up every hour?"

Sound familiar? Are you a complainer? If so—STOP!

People that complain suck the life right out of you and nobody will want to be around you. People who complain about everything but make no effort to change their ways, sadden Me. Criticizing and complaining show little Christ-like life.

I gave you a brain and creativity. Use it! Don't complain. Get busy and make changes and help your friends who are like this stop it, too.

When you complain that shows Me you are not happy with what I have given you and you don't trust Me. Complaining is not a fruit of the Spirit and is detrimental to the peace, joy, and patience that I give you.

Philippians 2:14 *Do all things without grumbling or arguing.* (CSB)

October 16

ONE HUNDRED REASONS TO SMILE

When life gives you a hundred reasons to break down and cry and you feel sorry for yourself—get tough and show this thing called life that you have one hundred reasons to smile and be thankful.

We all know someone who wallows in self-pity. In fact, each of us has had times when we felt sorry for ourselves. Your circumstances are bad---nobody likes you--- and no matter what you do, you can never do it right.

Thinking like this is selfish and wrong. Self-pity shows a lack of trust in God. The cure for self-pity is to quit looking inward. Rather than looking inward or outward, look upward. This is the one and only way to rid yourself of self-pity, and be happy.

God will take care of everything in His time.

Psalm 73:23 *Yet I am always with you; you hold me by my right hand.* (NIV)

October 17

PRAYER IS OUR DIRECT LINE WITH HEAVEN

God will lead you where He wants you to be, but you have to talk to Him daily to see where He wants you to go. The only way to get the answer is through prayer.

Prayer is our direct line with Heaven. It is a communication process that allows us to talk to God directly. Praying is talking to your best friend. When you pray--- pray with worship, reverence, and faith.

Prayer is the exercise of faith and hope. It is the privilege of touching the heart of the Father through the Son of God, but also to listen to what He is saying.

Know with assurance that God hears you when you pray.

Hebrews 11:6 *So you see, it is impossible to please God without faith. Anyone who wants to come to him must believe that there is a God and that he rewards those who sincerely seek him. (NLT)*

October 18

THE LOVE OF MONEY

The world is filled with greed, larceny, and lust. Most people are consumed with the love of money and what it can bring them.

They believe the more they obtain, the happier they will be; but this is not true. Money is the root of evil. It makes people steal, kill, and is a major temptation that can become a terrible master.

It is not a sin to be wealthy, but those blessed with wealth should share generously with the less fortunate. Wealth is a gift from God, entrusted to carry out His work on earth.

God owns everything you have--- it is His—it is only entrusted to you. None of the money or material things are yours to keep permanently.

There has never been anyone buried with his wealth and material things he accumulated in life.

Matthew 6:24 *No one can serve two masters. Either you will hate the one and love the other, or you will be devoted to the one and despise the other. You cannot serve both God and Money. (NIV)*

October 19

THE POWER OF POSITIVE THINKING

Staying positive doesn't mean that things will turn out okay. Rather, it's knowing that you will be okay, no matter how things turn out.

God gave us a free will on whether to accept Him in our lives or not. He chose to create and allow us to live freely in our thoughts and minds. The characteristic of God shows how truly blessed we are and should make our attitude towards others be positive.

There will be situations in life that will bring you down, such as the loss of a job, relationship problems, or an illness that can steal the love and joy from your life. Satan is using the evil and negative things of the world to discourage you. You need to stay focused on the only one who can conquer negativity—Jesus Christ, our Lord.

There is power in positive thinking, and for the believer it is rooted in what you believe about God and His word.

Matthew 6:33 *But if thine eyes are unhealthy, your whole body will be full of darkness. (KJV)*

October 20

THINK BEFORE YOU SPEAK

Sticks and stones can break your bones, but names will never hurt you. This is so untrue.

Choose your words wisely before you speak. Choosing the right words to live by is a test for all of us.

If you think before you speak you could stop a lot of unnecessary pain. Say your words in a kind way, for the truth is the truth and people will have to accept it.

The tongue is a two-edged sword and can do much harm when used inappropriately.

Before you speak ask yourself 3 things:

1) Is it true?
2) Is it necessary?
3) Is it kind?

The misuse of our tongues seems to add intrigue and destruction. We need to get back to basic principles of recognizing the good and not the bad in others.

Proverbs 12:18 *The words of the reckless pierce like swords, but the tongue of the wise brings healing. (NIV)*

October 21

WHAT IS A TRUE FRIEND?

Friendships are important---especially to women. You can have a lot of acquaintances, but finding a true friend is like finding a needle in a haystack.

Casual friendships are those you may chat with on topics, such as a new book or new fashion. Most women are blessed with having one or two really good friends—the kind who will always be there for you--- no matter what!

These are the people who truly care how you are, want to share the good and bad times with you, and will always have a shoulder for you to cry on.

A true friend is one who asks how you are---and waits for the answer.

Proverbs 12:26 *One who is righteous is a guide to his neighbor, but the way of the wicked leads them astray. (ESV)*

October 22

BE YOURSELF!

As Fashion Icon Coco Chanel once said, "Beauty begins the moment you decide to be yourself."

Remember, true beauty comes out when you learn to be yourself and not try to be someone else. There are many fake people in the world: They wear a fake face, a fake mask and a fake body that will fade in time. However, a true character will always leave your soul looking beautiful.

So don't worry about what anyone has to say about you, be who you are and be proud.

Genesis 1:27 *So God created mankind in his own image, in the image of God he created them; male and female, he created them. (NIV)*

October 23

THE LOSS OF A CHILD

One of the largest and most devastating things a person can endure is losing one's child. It is the loneliest, most desolate journey a person can endure in her or his life. It is the ultimate tragedy.

It's also heart-wrenching when you lose a pet. If you own one, the average life span depending on the type of pet is anywhere from 5 to 15 years.

As a parent you gave birth to life as a promise to the future. The relationship between parents and their children is among the most intense in life.

We question God why He allows this tragedy. The answer is "We won't know until we get to heaven." Remember—God has a plan. We were all created by God and are His children. When He takes a child to Heaven it is a very loving thing. Perhaps He saved this child from some horrible pain he might have experienced in life?

Know you will be reunited with your child one day and learn the answer of why this tragedy occurred.

Revelation 7:16-17 *They shall hunger no more, neither thirst anymore; the sun shall not strike them, nor any scorching heat. (ESV)*

October 24

LET CHRIST LEAD YOU

TAKE MY HAND, WE WILL GET THROUGH THIS TOGETHER. As a child of mine you should fear nothing for when you are in My hands, I will guide you through every tough situation and direct you on the right path.

Allow Me to lead you. Follow the Holy Spirit and don't turn away from My will. Trust that I will lead you out of the dark and into the peaceful light.

HOLD ON! Keep seeking Me and believe in Me, for I will always hear and answer your prayers.

For I, the Lord, will hold the right hand, saying unto thee: Fear not, I will help thee." (Isaiah 41:13 KJV)

Isaiah 41:10 *Fear thou not; for I am with thee: be not dismayed, for I am thy God. I will strengthen yea, I will help thee; yea, I will uphold thee with the right hand of my righteousness. (KJV)*

October 25

TRIALS IN YOUR LIFE

God never said that the journey would be easy, but He did say that the arrival would be worthwhile.

In your life you will have many trials. Expect them, but you don't have to face them alone. While going through it, it seems like it will never end.

But God is omnipotent and God all of the time. He knows exactly how long this trial in your life will last and He will give you strength to get through them.

Trials have a way of wearing us down and before long we think we cannot go on. The enemy of our soul whispers that we are alone and we will never make it. Be strong and courageous, for God is by your side.

The peace God gives us is a peace that will settle our hearts and give our minds rest.

Isaiah 43:2 *When you go through deep waters, I will be with you. (NLT)*

October 26

GOD CLOSES THE DOOR

Until God opens the next door, praise Him in the hallway. When God shuts a door, it's because He's only going to open another door that's BIGGER and BETTER for you.

The first closed doors known in the stories of Scripture are the gates of Paradise in The Garden of Eden. After Adam and Eve broke God's only commandment to them they were forced to leave Paradise. Now, that's a closed door!

He has a reason for everything He does. We just have to accept that a door is closed and we many never know the reason.

God closes a door to reveal something about our relationship with Him. Seek refuge and direction and you will get an answer!

***Jeremiah* 32:27** *Behold I am the Lord, the God of all flesh. Is anything too difficult for Me? (KJV)*

October 27

KEEP FOCUSED

It's easy to be distracted everyday on what's important. Keeping your eyes focused on what really matters is difficult because we are faced with problems, heartaches, and disappointments that are thrown at us by the devil.

The only way to battle through and conquer this is through faith. The Apostle Peter decided to walk on water after Jesus told him he could do it. Peter forgot who was keeping him afloat and began thinking about the reasons he should be sinking---and he did!

We have to keep our eyes focused on Jesus, not on our troubles, for He can get you through the strongest storm and bring you out on the other side.

Matthew 14:30 *But when he looked around at the high waves, he was terrified and began to sink. "Save me, Lord!" he shouted. (TLB)*

October 28

WHEN DIVORCE IS OK

Christians believe in emulating the life of Jesus Christ Himself. They believe this is the way to heaven and the Holy Bible is the ultimate source to do it.

What does the Bible say about divorce? In the Old Testament Moses allows a man to divorce his wife if she has done something indecent.

Divorce is allowed if adultery is involved; however, what the Bible says about divorce in the New Testament is different. Jesus is clear that marriage is a lifetime relationship and there is no such thing as divorce.

But if a Christian is married to a non-Christian and they divorce, the Christian spouse may marry again. Christianity is a forgiving religion and one should not turn against one who divorces. As long as you repent, you will be forgiven, for our God is a forgiving God.

Psalm 147:3 *He heals the brokenhearted and binds up their wounds. (NIV)*

October 29

THE 5 SENSES

When God created us He gave us 5 extra senses. A sense is a physiological capacity of organisms that provide perception. The 5 senses are: Feel, Taste, Sound, Smell and Sight. Through these we understand and perceive the world around us.

We should never take any of these gifts for granted. The gift of **sight** enables us to see the beautiful things around us. With the gift of **sound** we are able to communicate with others, and by **touching** we can feel things such as a pet or another person. When we **smell** we send signals to the brain that helps us detect if something is poisonous or pleasant, and by **tasting** we can enjoy the basic tastes of sweet, bitter, salty, or sour.

God gave us these so we can experience Him with all our senses---To be able to connect with Him and the rest of His creation.

Take time each day to thank Him for these 5 gifts He has given you. Be thankful for your sight, hearing, touch, smell and taste, for they are priceless.

Proverbs 20:12 *The hearing ear and the seeing eye, the Lord has made them both. (KJV)*

October 30

REJECTION

No one likes to be rejected. Unfortunately, we all will experience rejection at some time in our life. The number of people who are affected by rejection is staggering.

Husbands leave loyal wives, and hard-working employees get passed over for promotions. Rejection wounds us deeply because it attacks the person we are. It destroys our self-esteem and attacks our purpose in life.

We were created to be loved, accepted and appreciated. Rejection is an anti-Christ spirit that starves a person from love and acceptance. The root of rejection is actually incredibly simple: Damage from rejection is the result of a misplaced identity.

You need to start seeing yourself for who you are in Christ and the person that God has really formed within you.

Some helpful ways to do this is:

1) To love yourself
2) Have a thankful heart
3) Have a loving relationship with Jesus.

For believers it is our position in Christ to know that when we are born again, we are accepted. Even though we do not deserve it, Christ has blessed us with spiritual blessing; therefore if you are a child of God you may suffer a disappointment in life, but remember, as a child of the King, this rejection is only a bump in the road.

Psalm 27:10 *When my father and my mother forsake me, then the Lord will take me up. (KJV)*

October 31

HERE TODAY---GONE TOMORROW

Growing up my mother told me, "Life is fleeting. You are here today and gone tomorrow." She was right, for the years flew by quickly.

When you are little you think you're going to live forever. You can't wait until you're 16 so you can drive a car; then 21 so you're able to vote and drink alcohol. Then the years fly by and you wake up one day and look in the mirror.

You're shocked at the reflection you see for looking back is someone who has wrinkles and graying hair. Where did the time go?

You start reminiscing about the good and bad times you experienced through the years. The people you loved who are no longer here--- and how your life is today.

Some people are content, while others are regretful. But the things that happened to you were supposed to happen—nothing was a coincidence.

Your life went exactly like it was supposed to. You were never in control---God was, and He still is!

Start by accepting this and know that He is watching over you and will never leave you. Your life is a lesson—one that you will learn from and prepare you for the ultimate ending: Living in eternity with your Father in Heaven.

Psalm 27:1 *The Lord is my light and my salvation. Whom shall I fear? (KJV)*

NOVEMBER

November 1

THIS TOO SHALL PASS

Cast your cares and troubles to me. Worrying about things is a waste of precious time. What is going to happen is supposed to happen. There is nothing you can do to change the outcome, so why add unnecessary anxiety when you should be enjoying the precious day of today?

Every day is a gift from Me, so make it the best you can. Remember there is nothing you could do to change your circumstances. Enjoy the 'little' things in life, such as your loved ones, your health, the roof over your head and the food in the refrigerator.

You may think it is not enough, but have I ever let you down? You might have had times when money was scarce or a health scare, but in the end it all came out okay, so TRUST ME! Remember, no matter what you are going through now---"This too shall pass."

Matthew 6:33 *But seek first the kingdom of God and His righteousness, and all these things shall be given to you as well. (NIV)*

◆ November 2 ◆

WOMEN ARE MULTI-TASKERS

Women are multi-taskers. They are the champions at keeping all the balls juggling in the air, never dropping one.

But it's not easy!

Women have the responsibility of being in charge of the house, the children, and trying to squeeze a little time for themselves, while some even have 9 to 5 jobs.

How do they do it? They cannot do it without the help of God. When they feel like they are unraveling they go to the one person who holds it all together.

He is the only thing that can get them through the day. They don't turn to drugs, alcohol or any other vice that is a temporary pseudo solution.

When you feel like you can't go another day---PRAY! Ask your Father for faith and willpower to know, "This too shall pass."

He will never let you down.

Philippians 4:19 *My God will meet all your needs according to the riches of his glory in Christ Jesus. (NIV)*

November 3

STANDING UP AGAINST YOUR ENEMIES AND FRIENDS

It takes a lot of courage to make a stand and go up against your enemies. But what happens when it's your friends that you have to stand up against?

These are the times when it gets very hard to go against the grain and stand up for what you believe is right. This is where your will power is tested---seeing if you are strong enough to stick it out to the end.

Unfortunately, it may not end the way you hope for it may end up that you're not friends with those people anymore.

Speaking up for yourself is a learned habit—no one is born with it. You have to develop the skill.

John 15: 12-15 *This is my commandment, that you love one another as I have loved you. Greater love has no one than this, that someone lay down his life for his friends. (ESV)*

November 4

BE THE BEST VERSION OF YOURSELF

The power you have is to be the best version of yourself you can be, so you can create a better world. Being the best version, takes time and effort. You really never know what your best version is until you start to become it.

Once you work on improving yourself, you'll discover a new way to get better, and it becomes a continual process.

Colossians 3: 23 *Whatever you do, work heartily, as for the Lord and not for men, knowing that from the Lord you will receive the inheritance as your reward. You are serving the Lord Christ. (ESV)*

November 5

YOU ARE BLESSED

When life gets overwhelming we tend to forget the things we are blessed with. Dealing with relationship problems, raising a family, and juggling finances can be difficult and take joy away from our life. The last thing on our mind is feeling we are blessed and give thanks.

When we are stressed we forget to appreciate the small things. We may forget to say thank you to someone who went far and beyond, or thank God for what He has given us.

Don't let the gratefulness diminish your joy anymore. Proverbs tells us by the fruit of our lips our stomach is filled. You are what you speak.

The next time you want to say something—stop and think before you speak.

Romans 5:3-5 *More than that, we rejoice in our sufferings, knowing that suffering produces endurance and endurance produces character and character produces hope and hope does not put us to shame, because God's love has been poured into our hearts through the Holy Spirit who has been given to us. (RSV)*

November 6

DON'T BE NEEDY!

People want to be liked by others. When you are in school you want to be 'the most popular,' for when you're liked you will get the best dates and coolest friends.

But being liked by everyone is so overrated. It's much better to have God's approval and love of others from a genuine place, instead of neediness.

A true Christian will not be the most popular for the most popular do things that are contrary to the Christian lifestyle. As a child of God we are not to join evil but expose it, and people don't like others pining out and telling them to turn away from their sins.

We are not to live for the world to try to impress others or do better than others. Christians live for Christ putting Him first in everything they do.

Romans 12:2 *And be not conformed to this world but be transformed by the renewing of your mind, that ye may prove what is that good, and acceptable, and perfect will of God. (KJ)*

November 7

KEEP ON DREAMING

Everybody has a dream. Some dreams come true, while others never come to fruition. It's okay to dream, but you must keep things in perspective and not wish for something that is impossible to reach.

Perhaps it is a dream of starting your own ministry, or going back to school even at a ripe age to launch a new career.

Along the way you will be confronted with problems and roadblocks that arise.

Many people will give up just before they reach their goal, never making that dream into a reality. These 'dreams' are put into your heart and mind from God and He gives you nothing that you can't do---with His help!

Depend on God to help you reach the goal---He will be your guide. God speaks to us through dreams and visions. He actively speaks to us through them to bring instruction. We just have to be open to listening to what He is saying.

Joel 2:28 *And it shall come to pass afterward, that I will pour out my Spirit on all flesh; your sons and your daughters shall prophesy, your old men shall dream dreams and your young men shall see visions. (KJV)*

November 8

THOU SHALT NOT MAKE UNTO THEE ANY GRAVEN IMAGE

This is the second commandment and together with the other nine given by God to Moses at Mount Sinai.

This teaches us that we must worship God as He truly is. God cannot be an idol made by man----He is Spirit. You are not to worship anything other than Him.

That includes worshiping another person or material things. Bowing before an idol to pay homage to one's own image of God may appear to be an act of great devotion, but it is ignorant of God's purpose for mankind. An idol is whatever you value most in life.

It is very hard to obey all Ten Commandments but God knows what's best for us, and that is the purpose for the Second Commandment and all the others. Make sure that you do not allow anything in life to become more valuable that God, for He is infinitely valuable and beautiful and desires that we all come to saving faith in Jesus Christ.

Matthew 22:37 *Love the Lord your God with all your heart and with all your soul and with all your mind. (ESV)*

November 9

WITH GOD BESIDE YOU, WHO CAN BE AGAINST YOU?

"Do not be afraid for I have ransomed you. I have called you by name. You are mine when you go through deep waters. I will be with you when you go through rivers of difficulty. You will not drown when you walk through the fires of depression. You will not be burned up. The flames will not consume you for I am the Lord your God." (NLT)

Isaiah 43: 1-3

What inspiring and uplifting words from our Lord. Whenever you are having a bad day or going through a difficult time in your life, remember this. With God besides you---who can be against you?

Deuteronomy 31:8 *It is the Lord who goes before you. He will be with you; he will not leave you or forsake you. Do not fear or be dismayed. (ESV)*

November 10

SET UP BOUNDARIES

God determines who walks into your life. It's up to you to decide who you let walk away, and who you let stay. Personal boundaries are talked about in the Bible. It states that our life would be a mess unless we set these boundaries.

Your body, thoughts and relationships should belong to you.

Without boundaries you will be led astray by the wrong people who want to control you, and without boundaries you will be exposed to temptations that could be avoided.

The Bible reminds us that we have the right to say "no" or "yes" to things that are bad or good. Don't be forced or pushed into doing something you will be sorry for later.

Timothy 4:16 *Keep a close watch on yourself and on the teaching. Persist in this for by doing so you will save yourself and your hearers. (ESV)*

November 11

HOLD YOUR HEAD UP HIGH

Never bend your head down. Always hold it up high. Look at the world straight in the eye. Don't let people and the ways of the world bring you down.

Life can be cruel and strange but always remember there is a rainbow at the end of a storm. Keeping your head up when you feel unable of doing so is the trick that makes the difference between winners and losers.

Things are never as easy as we would like and many conditions of life escape our control---that is why learning to cope with failure and disappointment is very important for our sanity.

John 6:53 *So Jesus said to them, "Truly, truly I say to you, unless you eat the flesh of the Son of Man and drink his blood, you have no life in you."* (ESV)

November 12

WITH GOD ALL THINGS ARE POSSIBLE

You say, "It's impossible." God says, "With me all things are possible."

You say, "I'm exhausted." He says, "Wait on me. I will renew your strength."

You say, "I can't do it." He says, "You can do all things through Me."

You say, "It's not worth it." He says, "It will be---just keep going."

You say, "I can't forgive myself." He says, "You can—because I have."

Never give up for with God beside you will get you through the impossible.

Psalm 55:22 *Cast your cares on the Lord and he will sustain you; he will never let the righteous be shaken.* (NIV)

EMERGENCY NUMBERS TO MEMORIZE

EMERGENCY NUMBERS YOU MUST REMEMBER

When in Sorrow..........John 14
When man disappoints you..........Psalm 27
When you have sinned..........Psalm 51
When you worry..........Matthew 6:19-34
When God seems far away..........Psalm 139
When you are lonely and fearful..........Psalm 23
When you want peace and rest..........Matthew 11:25-30
When the world seems bigger than God is..........Psalm 90
If you want to be fruitful..........John 15
When people seem unkind..........John 15
When you want to get along with your fellowman..........Romans 12
When you are in danger..........Psalm 91

Available 24/7 Phone is not needed. Operator Available 24 Hours a day named God.

Isaiah 41:10 *Fear not, for I am with you; be not dismayed, for I am your God; I will strengthen you, I will help you, I will uphold you with my righteous right hand. (NKJV)*

November 14

5 BIBLE VERSES A WOMAN SHOULD KNOW

1) I will praise thee: for I am fearfully and wonderfully made.
   Psalm 139:14

2) Above all else, guard your heart for everything you do flows from it.
   Proverbs 4:23

3) She opens her mouth with wisdom, and the teaching of kindness is on her tongue.
   Proverbs 31:26

4) You are all together beautiful, my love, there is no flaw in you.
   Song of Solomon 4:7

5) For we are God's masterpiece. He has created us anew in Christ Jesus, so we can do the good things he planned for us long ago.
   Ephesians 2:10

Genesis 2:18 *Then the Lord God said, "It is not good that the man should be alone; I will make him a helper fit for him."* (ESV)

November 15

PERFECTION

Throughout Scripture God says to be perfect. He is the standard for perfection. But being human, there is nobody who is perfect. God has every right to throw us into hell for eternity, and He should. But out of His love for us He brought His perfect son to become perfection on our behalf.

So the next time you feel inferior, remember:

Sara was Impatient
Elijah was Moody
Zaccheus was Short
Lazarus was dead
Paul was a Murderer
Matha was a Worrier
Mirima was a Gossip
Jacob was a Cheater
Peter had a Temper
David had an Affair
Noah was a Drunk
Jonah ran from God
Moses stuttered

Ephesians 1:7 *But in Christ we have redemption through His blood, the forgiveness of our trespasses, according to the riches of His grace. (NIV)*

November 16

LIFE IN HEAVEN

It is hard to imagine what life will be like in Heaven. Nobody has ever returned to tell us, but we have faith that it will be beyond words to describe.

Waiting for us when we enter will be our loved ones who have passed before us, or perhaps your favorite pet that you miss so much—running to give you puppy dog kisses?

I can only imagine!

Surrounded by His glory what will my heart feel? Will I dance for Jesus or be in awe that I will be completely still? Will I stand in His presence or fall to my knees and sing hallelujah or will I be able to speak at all?

I can only imagine!

Revelation 21:4 *He will wipe every tear from their eyes and death shall be no more, neither shall there be mourning, nor crying, nor pain anymore, for the former things have passed away. (ESV*

November 17

GOD SENDS US ANGELS

Some people are angels who leave a hint of heaven wherever they go. God sends us angels in times when we most need them.

We live in a mysterious, spiritual world. In the Bible it talks when God sent an angel to reveal something. He sent Zecchariah, the father of John the Baptist, to tell him his wife, Elizabeth, would have a son; and God sent an angel to Mary, telling her she was chosen to give birth to the Savior.

Angels appeared to many of the prophets in Biblical times and they are sent to us today to watch over us. They are sent by God to protect, encourage, and strengthen us. Angels are God's servants that are sent into the world to serve His will.

They do not have to appear wearing white feather wings. Angels can appear to us in the form of a friend or someone who is in our life to help us through a bad time. It is far more common for angels to appear in physical form as humans as a good Samaritan who stops to help you change your tire or another patient in the hospital waiting room, who said kind words or held your hand while you waited for news.

Angels who appear to us in physical form have very kind eyes and a peaceful calming energy. They are extremely helpful and usually don't have to say much—though what they do say is very poignant.

Psalm 91:11-12 *For He will command His angels concerning you to guard you in all your ways. On their hands they will bear you up, lest you strike your foot against a stone. (NKJV)*

November 18

DON'T JUDGE A BOOK BY ITS COVER

Looks are so important to many people. They judge others by how they appear—if they are overweight or too thin they criticize them, making them feel inferior and insecure.

Nobody should criticize anyone for there is not one person who is perfect. Even the most beautiful movie star will grow old and lose his or her looks.

We all have flaws and need to look at a person's interior. How their heart speaks and if they are compassionate, loyal, and kind.

God thinks you're beautiful because of who you are to Him---His child!

Remember, no matter how you feel about yourself, God thinks you are beautiful! Isn't that enough?

***Song of Soloman* 4:7** *You are altogether beautiful. My love, there is no flaw in you.* (NIV)

◆ November 19 ◆

A GODLY MAN

Any man can make a woman happy by buying her expensive things or complimenting her; but a man who prays and is a believer will fully complete her into becoming the woman she was created to be.

A Godless man will belittle, control, manipulate and degrade the woman because he is not filled with the Holy Spirit, but instead with worldly things.

These men are misogynists, narcissists and hypocrites who think only of themselves.

If you are in a relationship with this type of man, remove yourself from the situation or you will never find happiness and peace. Find a man who loves God first and you second.

Deuteronomy 22:10 *Don't plow an ox with a donkey together.*
If the two of you don't agree on your faith, you are likely to encounter difficulties. (ESV)

◆ November 20 ◆

A STORY WRITTEN BY THE FINGER OF GOD

History is a story written by the finger of God.

God is the Creator and is sovereign over mankind. Whatever happens in your life was ordained to come to pass by God. Even evil things can be used for good.

Whatever happens is what God planned to happen. Prophecy is history written ahead of time before it ever happens. If you know anything about God and His Word, you know nothing happens that God does not know will happen.

He determines history before it happens and what God ordained to come to pass can't be changed. The outcome has already been determined, so quit worrying about things you have no power over and know that God has it handled!

Romans 8:28 *And we know that all things work together for good to them that love God, to them who are called according to his purpose. (KJV)*

November 21

LIFE IS A RAT RACE

Life is difficult. Everyday is a race you must run and in a race only one can come in first. As a believer you must never give up. Run until you see the finish line. Your Lord and Savior is the prize waiting for you every step of the way.

Thankfully, the race you will be running depends not on human will or exertion, but on God who has mercy. When running the race of life choose to not give up on God because He never gives up on you!

Hebrews 12:1 *Therefore, since we are surrounded by such a great cloud of witnesses, let us throw off everything that hinders and the sin that so easily entangles. (NIV)*

November 22

WHAT IS FAITH?

Faith. What is it? Faith is taking the first step, even when you don't see the whole staircase. It is a reality that gives substance to things before they become visible to the natural eye.

The Bible says that faith is a complete trust or confidence in someone or something. Without faith we have no place with God, and it is impossible to please Him.

Faith is not something we conjure up on our own, nor is it something we are born with or money can buy. It is truly a gift from God, not because we deserve it, have earned it, or are worthy of it.

It is simply given to us from God along with His grace and mercy according to His holy plan and purpose.

Faith comes by hearing the Word and hearing through the word of Christ. Romans 10:17

Hebrew 11:6 *And without faith it is impossible to please Him, for whoever would draw near to God must believe that He exists and that He rewards those who seek Him. (ESV)*

November 23

TURN YOUR ENEMY INTO YOUR FRIEND

The best way to destroy an enemy is to turn him into a friend. Jesus died for us while we were ungodly, wicked sinners who were his enemies, so we should do nothing less than do good to those who hate us and do bad to us.

We must pray for our enemies so that God would not only bless them but that He might also save them. We were once enemies that Jesus died for, so how can we not pray for those who persecute us?

Love your enemies, do good to them that hate you, ask God to bless those who curse you, and to pray for those who hate you.

Matthew 5:44 *But I say unto you, Love your enemies, bless them that curse you, do good to them that hate you and pray for them which despitefully use you and persecute you. (KJV)*

November 24

YOU CAN DO IT!

"I CAN"
"I WILL"
"I AM"

Do not be upset when you fail at something. Anyone who has ever achieved anything, failed many times before succeeding.

Failing teaches us valuable lessons that lead to success.

In the Bible it says "You can do all things through Christ who strengthens you." (Philippians 4:13 NKJV)

Yes, you can do anything as long as you have God. Without Him things will be difficult and impossible. God runs everything in your life. He has planned every day of the life of each of us before He even created the earth. He watches over and guides us in the right direction.

If you are sick---He is the greatest physician
If you are weak---He is your strength
If you're fearful--- He is your peace.

Romans 11:36 *For of Him, and through Him, and to Him are all things, to him be glory forever! Amen (NKJV)*

◆ November 25 ◆

YOU ARE A MASTERPIECE

"God loves each one of us as if there were only one of us."
Augustine

When we were created we were all made different but in the image of our Father.

There are not 2 people alike---even with fraternal or identical twins. God did this on purpose because he only makes masterpieces.

Knowing that we are unique should humble you, because you are an original.

He did not make us as a mass production—He took great care in making us who we were meant to be. With that said, never try to look or be like somebody else.

There will be times when you feel like anything but a masterpiece, but the Lord wants you to know how much He loves you and He is with you even in times of despair.

Jeremiah 1:5 *"Before I formed thee in the belly I knew thee, and before thou camest forth out of the womb, I sanctified thee." (KJV)*

◆ November 26 ◆

CHRIST LITERALLY WALKED IN OUR SHOES

Jesus was a perfect, sinless Man who walked in the ways of His Father. This gives us hope.

Yes, He faced his fair share of heartbreak, ridicule, mockery and betrayal—just as we have all experienced.

Jesus grieved the loss of someone He loved. He was betrayed by others and was mocked and beaten, before He was carried away to be crucified—for you and me!

He once walked this earth and knows what you are going through. You can rest assure that He will deliver you from the fire and pain you are facing now. There is absolutely nothing that you will go through in life that He cannot heal. Cling to His words and He will pull you through because "He has walked in your shoes!"

1 John 2:3-6 *And by this we know that we have come to know him, if we keep his commandments. (ESV)*

◆ November 27 ◆

GOD'S PROMISE

"We may speak about a place where there are no tears, no death, no fear, no night; but Heaven. The beauty of Heaven is seeing God."
Max Lucado

As Apostle John received a revelation about end times and what Heaven would be like, he heard a loud voice coming from the throne in the New Jerusalem saying, "He will wipe away every tear from their eyes, and death shall be no more, neither shall there be mourning, nor crying, nor pain anymore, for the former things have passed away."

Doesn't this sound wonderful?

The promise of no more tears or crying will be after the end of the world, after the Great White Throne Judgment, and there will be no more suffering on earth.

Though you cannot see Him yet, believe in Him and rejoice with joy that it is inexpressible and filled with glory of what is waiting for you when you are called home.

Isaiah 66:22-24 *For as the new heavens and the new earth that I make shall remain before me, says the Lord, so shall your offspring and your name remain. (KJV)*

November 28

IF YOU CAN'T FLY, THEN RUN

Martin Luther King, an American clergyman and civil rights leader known for his use of nonviolence and civil disobedience was assassinated at age 39.

Mr. King said something once that always impacted me.

"If you can't fly, then run. If you can't run, then walk. If you can't walk then crawl, but whatever you do you have to keep moving forward."

Whether it's moving on from a relationship, past sin or disappointments, God has a plan for you. His plan for you is not in the past—it's in the future. Keep your eye what's in front of you—not behind. Allow the love of God to compel you to keep moving forward and don't look back.

Philippians 3:14 *I press on toward the mark for the prize of high calling of God in Christ Jesus. (KJV)*

◆ November 29 ◆

GIRL POWER!

God made woman to be strong, confident, and courageous. Contrary to the belief that the world is male-dominated, it is the woman who provides the foundation of a family. She accomplishes this through grace, wisdom, justice, creativity and hope.

It is the woman who is known to have better intuition, patience, emotional focus, and compassion. God created woman to be the most incredible balance of soft and strong. It can be exhausting being a woman for she has to be a mother, wife, daughter, friend and sister.

Never allow anyone to make you feel inadequate and less of the wonderful person you were created to be. And as you age, it shouldn't bother you because the best tunes are played on the oldest fiddles.

Be the attitude you want to be around.

Titus 2:3-5 *Older women likewise are to be reverent in behavior, not slanders or slaves to much wine. They are to teach what is good, and so train the young women to love their husbands and children, to be self-controlled, pure, working at home, kind and submissive to their own husbands, that the word of God may not be reviled. (ESV)*

November 30

FINDING YOURSELF

Do you feel lost, alone, and there's no reason to go on living? Quit feeling sorry and go out there and find yourself!

You aren't a crumbled up dollar bill you found buried in your coat pocket.

The real you is hiding under cultural conditioning, others peoples opinions, and inaccurate conclusions that were stamped in your mind as a child about who you are.

Finding yourself is really returning to the real you---the person you were before the world got its hands on you.

But you are never really lost if you are a child of God, for He is always by your side.

Jeremiah 1:5 *Before I formed thee in the belly I knew thee; and before thou camest forth out of the womb I sanctified thee and I ordained thee a prophet unto the nations. (KJV)*

DECEMBER

December 1

THERE IS NO SUCH THING AS LUCK

You question why some people seem to have it all. They have looks, money, and everything they touch seems to turn to gold.

You say they were born lucky. But there is no such thing as luck. Everything that happens is supposed to happen. In the Bible it teaches that there is no such thing as luck—but instead, blessings.

We wish 'good luck' to someone taking a test and we wish ourselves luck when we roll a dice or spin a wheel in an arcade, but as a Christian you believe in God who is in control of our future. He is in total control and our life is not controlled by chance or luck.

Since luck means accidental good fortune—God and luck simply don't go hand-in-hand.

Do not be envious of others for you don't know what they face behind closed doors.

Bad things that happen to us, work out for the good in the end. God is in charge and He alone knows and has control over all things past, present, and future.

Proverbs 16:1 *We can gather our thoughts, but the Lord gives the right answer. (NLT)*

◆ December 2 ◆

KEEP FROM HURTING OTHERS

The most costly liquid in the universe is a tear. It consists of 1% water and 99% feelings. Think before you say something and hurt someone!

Scripture teaches us to love one another and not to harm your neighbor. We are not to hurt others physically or emotionally.

Ironically, the most harmful weapon does not weigh an ounce—it is mere words. Words can tear one down. Slander, gossip, and lying, are all evil. Words can scar you more than a physical blow. The tongue has no bones, but is strong enough to break a person's heart.

5 things you need to remember as not to hurt a person's feelings:

1) **They are not you**. People have different experiences, beliefs and values. You cannot expect them to behave like you would in the same situation.
2) **Some words are just socially negative**. Before you call someone fat, etc., ask yourself if the words you use are kind, and joyful.
3) **Avoid Uncomfortable topics.** Politics, religions, health concerns and intimacy issues are all topics that have unease and emotional sensitivity associated with them. Let the other person have privacy on these topics, unless they engage you first.
4) **You aren't perfect either!** No one is perfect and we all make mistakes.
5) **Avoid Talking About Physical Appearance.** Others are still worthy of our respect no matter their appearance.

Romans 12:17 *Do not repay anyone for evil. Be careful to do what is right in the eyes of everyone. (NIV)*

December 3

CHILDREN ARE A BLESSING

A child is truly a gift from God. Jesus loved children for they are innocent and pure. Your child will be your best friend until the day you are called home. Of course there will be trying times along the way when you butt heads and say unkind words to one another that you will forever be sorry for, but the love between a mother and child is the strongest and unconditional love of all.

Jesus loved his mother, Mary, with all His heart. As He was dying on the cross He was worried about His mother and who was going to take care of her. He made plans for her provision by putting one of the disciples in charge of her care.

Below is a beautiful saying from a mother to her child.

FOR MY CHILD (For my son, Joe)

I wish you the strength to face challenges with confidence. I wish you the wisdom as you adventure on your journey through life.

May you always stop to help someone along the way and listen to your heart to take risks.

You never have to win my love for it is unconditional and eternal. My love for you will never end---it is there from beginning to end.

Proverbs 31:26-27 *She opens her mouth with wisdom, and the teaching of kindness is on her tongue. She looks well to the ways of her household and does not eat the bread of idleness. (ESV)*

December 4

DON'T PLAY THE 'NOT' GAME

Not every day is a good day---There will be many days you wish were over. But you must show up anyway.

Not everyone tells the truth---Even a little white lie can be hurtful. You must trust anyway.

Not everyone will love you back---Those who you love the most may not love you the same. You must love them anyway.

Not every game will be played fair---There will be people who cheat to get ahead, but play anyway, because you can't win if you don't play.

Who said life would be fair and easy? You are alive and God wants you to make the best while you are here. Be positive and know that whatever you are going through----"This too shall pass."

Mark 9:23 *And Jesus said to him, "If you can! All things are possible for him who believes." (NASB)*

December 5

YOU ONLY LIVE AND DIE ONCE!

Although this is true… that man will only live once…. the truth is you only die once, too! With this said, you should live every single day like it's your last one, for it just may be.

Quit complaining and being negative! Whatever you have, thank God for. Things can always be worse. Yes, there are others that have more than you do, but there are those who also have less.

While you are living and breathing, be thankful for your loved ones and things you have in your life. God does not want you to waste your life away: He wants you to live with a purpose, and in order to do that you must forget your past and face the present.

Seize the moment and live life to the fullest!

John 6:47 *Truly, truly, I say to you, whoever believes has eternal life. I am the bread of life. (ESV)*

December 6

TURNING NEGATIVES INTO POSITIVES

Below are 3 Words That Can Turn Something Negative into a Positive

1) **FAIL**. A negative word that really means **F**irst **A**ttempt **I**n **L**earning.
   Failure is only a state of mind. You are only defeated if you think you are.

2) **END** is not the end. It means **E**ffort **N**ever **D**ies.
   As it says in the Bible—the end will come, but it is also the beginning of your new, everlasting life with God.

3) **NO**. Never take "no" for an answer for no really means
   Next **O**pportunity.
   Having to say 'no' to certain things, like a parent saying, 'no' to a child when they ask for something harmful can be life saving.

How words affect your brain will determine who you will become. Be an optimist and turn your life around into a positive, fulfilling one that others will want to copy.

***Thessalonians* 5:16-18** *Rejoice always, pray without ceasing, give thanks in all circumstances; for this is the will of God in Christ Jesus for you.* (NIV)

December 7

GOD'S SOVEREIGNTY

But God remembered Noah and all the beasts and all the cattle that were with him in the ark; and God caused a wind to pass over the earth and the water subsided. (Genesis 8:1 ESV)

God's sovereignty means that God is in charge of everything that happens in His universe. That means EVERYTHING!

Why does He allow bad things to happen?

Adversity, with its accompanying emotional pain comes to us in many forms.

Our suffering is under the control of an all-powerful and all-loving God. Our suffering has meaning and purpose.

Scripture teaches us that we must believe that God is completely sovereign, if we are to trust Him. The sovereignty of God is asserted—either expressly or implicitly, on almost every page of the Bible.

The Bible teaches that God not only created the universe, but that He upholds and sustains it day by day.

Don't question Why. He brings or allows into our lives only what is for His glory and our good.

Psalm 46:1 *God is our refuge and strength; an ever-present help in trouble.* (NAS)

December 8

STOP DOUBTING GOD

"Why do you doubt Me? Have you forgot that I am your Father, and as any Father, I will always protect and love you?"

These words come directly from God Himself, so why do we doubt Him? One reason is because we tend to expect positive results when we obey Him and when we don't get them we question Him.

Being human, we tend to have doubts, but lucky for us, God doesn't condemn us when we question Him, for He is big enough to handle our doubts and all our questions.

Even His closest disciple Peter doubted Jesus, and when he did, he fell in the water and almost drowned.

The problem was that Peter focused, like we do, on the waves and not the wave maker. By focusing on God and not our problems, we can stay afloat.

Isaiah 41:10 *So do not fear, for I am with you; do not be dismayed, for I am your God. I will strengthen you and help you. I will uphold you with my righteous right hand. (NIV)*

◆ December 9 ◆

BROKEN THINGS CAN BE FIXED

Do not be dismayed by the brokenness of the world today, for most things can break.

Remember, things that are broken can be fixed, especially when they are someone's feelings or relationships. These things cannot be mended with time, but with intention.

Go out and love intentionally, extravagantly, and unconditionally. This troubled, broken world waits in the darkness for the light that lies within you. You are a light worker who was sent to bring love and comfort to others.

Be the person who changes the world for the better!

Psalm 46:1 *God is our refuge and strength, an ever-present help in trouble.* (CSB)

December 10

THE THREE WISE MONKEYS

What a great message the three wise monkeys have: see no evil, speak no evil and hear no evil.

The first monkey, Mizaru, covers his eyes telling us that at times in your life you may see things that are unpleasant. Do not play out on what you see for seeing may be believing, but should not be.

The second monkey, Kikazaru, has his hands over his ears. People say things that may hurt you and they may be sorry for it afterwards. We may hear someone gossiping about another person and then repeat it, not knowing if it is true or not.

And the third monkey, Iwazaru, has his hands over his mouth, speaking no evil.

Many times we speak too quickly and say something we are sorry for later. Think before you speak! Words can destroy a person's life! ***Ephesians 4:29*** *Do not let any wholesome talk come out of your mouths, but only what is helpful for building others up according to their needs, that it may benefit those who listen.* (NIV)

Ephesians 4:29 *Do not let any wholesome talk come out of your mouths, but only what is helpful for building others up according to their needs, that it may benefit those who listen.* (NIV)

December 11

WOMEN ARE BUTTERFLIES

Women are fragile butterflies. When we are in our mother's womb we are protected (the cocoon.) As she gives birth and we emerge, the security we have known in the past nine months is taken away as we are introduced to the world.

As young children the perfect pureness we were born with becomes soiled by the things we may encounter; such as betrayal from the ones we love, sexual abuse or neglect.

When we are adults, unhealthy relationships can take away your self-esteem and worth. You withdrawl from the world and revert back into the womb where you felt safest.

But you can change this pattern and become the beautiful butterfly God created you to be. Break out of the cocoon: Be strong, know you are worthy, and that God will always love you.

Be the butterfly God made you to be, spread your wings and soar!

Psalm 46:5 *God is within her, she will not fall. (NIV)*

December 12

D-E-P-R-E-S-S-I-O-N ☹

Depression is a disease that millions of people experience. They can't be happy no matter what they have. Unfortunately, you cannot push a 'pause' button in your brain and there is no 'eject' button. Anxiety and depression is a mental illness and not a 'stage' that one goes through.

In the Bible it does not use the word depression, but instead downcast, sad, forlorn, discouraged and brokenhearted. Many people in the Bible showed the symptoms such as Moses, Hagar, Saul, David, Elijah and John the Baptist.

This disease can strike anyone and are normal parts of being human. But God is not angry with you for feeling this way. He is our hope when we feel this way. When you feel this way, fix your eyes on God and his power and love for you.

Psalm 34:18 *The Lord is close to the brokenhearted and saves those who are crushed in spirit. (NIV)*

December 13

YOU ARE A CHILD OF CHRIST!

When someone does something bad to you, don't seek revenge—rest assured, your enemies will get what's coming to them. God will deal with them. Leave it up to Him.

Unclench your fist, keep your mouth shut, and get rid of the anger inside.

Stand straight, take a deep breath and walk the path of righteousness. God will fight your battles.

Never forget who you are, but more important, whose you are. When someone starts tormenting, abusing, or messing with you, be still and know they are also messing with God.

2 Chronicles 20:17 *You will not have to fight his battle. Take up your positions; stand firm and see the deliverance the Lord will give you. Do not be afraid or discouraged. Go out to face them tomorrow and the Lord will be with you. (NIV)*

December 14

NO MORE SUFFERING

Everyone experiences pain sometime in their life. No one escapes difficult or hurtful situations. How you handle these difficulties says something about what kind of person you are and your opinion of God's sovereignty.

The secret is learning to accept the pain, and not allow it to control your life. By doing this, you show your trust in God's plan and love.

Some people allow the pain to consume their life, wallowing in their misery. Perhaps they enjoy the attention that suffering brings? Or perhaps it's because they don't know how to rest in the Lord?

Learn to let go of the pain knowing that God is in control of the situation and will get you through whatever situation it is. When you give it to God you will feel lighter and more at peace. Try it!

James 1:13 *When under trial, let no one say: "I am being tried by God." For with evil things God cannot be tried, nor does he himself try anyone.*

December 15

DO SOMETHING YOU LOVE

Your work is going to fill a big part of your life. The only way to really be successful and satisfied is to do something you love doing. Believe it is great and you are doing your best.

True happiness is not something you postpone for the future---it is something you design for the present.

Whether it is a job at a desk, with animals, working with the sick, or being a stay at home mother---- Be happy and give it your best, while thanking God.

Colossians 3:23 *Whatever you do, work at it with all your heart, as working for the Lord, not for human masters. (NIV)*

December 16

BE YOUR BROTHER'S KEEPER

If you can't be a light in someone's lives, don't be the darkness covering their dreams.

f you can't be the water to help their flowers grow, then don't be a pesticide to destroy it.

If you can't be a bridge to connect one another, then don't be the wall that separates them.

If you can't be the paintbrush to paint a pretty picture, then be the paint stripper to remove the sadness.

We can only be one another's keepers.

Galatians 6:2 *Bear ye one another's burdens, and so fulfill the law of Christ (ESV)*

December 17

THE IMPORTANCE OF WAITING ON GOD'S TIMING

God's delay is not his denial. If it seems slow in coming, wait patiently, for it will surely take place. It will not be delayed. (Habakkuk 2:3 NIV)

Everything that happens in your life will be on God's time. No matter how much you want it to happen now, if it is not His time, it will not happen.

One of the hardest things to do with the Lord is to wait on His timing to make certain things happen in people's lives.

God has a much slower time frame and a much slower way of working things out than we do. If you don't learn to adjust to His slower time frame we could easily get yourself knocked right out of what He has planned for you.

Trying to move ahead of God's timing with what He wants to do in a particular area of your life, you will find very quickly that everything will fall apart and unravel.

Isaiah 40:31 *But they who wait for the Lord shall renew their strength; they shall mount up with wings like eagles; they shall run and not be weary; they shall walk and not faint. (KJV)*

December 18

HUMILITY

Humility is the opposite of pride and as Christians, we are called to live humbly. But what does humble living really mean?

Pride is something that will never completely die, and being humble is a challenge that one must conquer time and time again in his or her lifetime.

Is humility thinking poorly about yourself, or is it more of focusing on Jesus and what He's done for you? Being humble is an attitude.

Meditate on this collection of thoughts about humility and what Jesus is saying to you.

2 Chronicles 7:14 *If my people who are called by my name humble themselves, and pray and seek my face and turn from their wicked ways, then I will hear from Heaven and will forgive their sin and heal their land. (KJV)*

December 19

ALWAYS BE HUMBLE

You are unique and under no obligation to be the person you once were. You have the right to follow your personal path and do what's best for you.

Stay true to yourself, but remain open to learn and change.

Never allow someone's criticism of you take you off your course to achieve your goals, and never think you are above anyone else—no matter how much you accumulate in life.

Always remain humble and thankful for what God has given you.

Ephesians 2:10 *For we are his workmanship, created in Christ Jesus for good works, which God prepared beforehand, that we should walk in them. (ESV)*

December 20

BE THE TYPE OF WOMAN THE DEVIL HATES

Be the type of woman the devil hates! Your Father in Heaven has given you great power that the enemy detests and he is constantly trying to take that power away from you.

Satan does not have the power of love, beauty and compassion, so when you display these acts, it infuriates him. The devil cannot bear that you don't worship him and that there is another creature (God) you do. Every time Satan sees you he sees God, for you are a reflection of Him.

The devil hates you so much because God loves you so much. You are the one creature that can destroy him by showing love and faith.

But don't waste your time focused on Satan's hate, but instead, spend it on feasting of God's love.

Be the kind of woman that when your feet hit the ground as you wake up, the devil says, "Oh crap, she's up!"

1 John 5:18-19 *We know that we are from God and the whole world lies in the power of the evil one. (ESV)*

December 21

YOU VS. GOD

You say, "I can't forgive myself for my mistakes."
God says, "You can… because I have." *Ephesians 4:32*

You say, "It's impossible."
God says, "With me all things are possible. *Luke 18:27*

You say, "I just can't make ends meet."
God says, "I will supply all your needs." *Philippians 4:19*

You say, "I'm afraid."
God says, "I didn't give you the spirit of fear, but of pwer."
Timothy 1:7

You say, "I can't handle anymore of this."
God says, "Give it to me. I'll carry it for you." *Psalm 55:22*

You say, "I'm not smart enough."
God says, "I'll give you wisdom." *1 Corinthians 1:30*

You say, "It's just not worth it."
God says, "It will be, just keep going." *Galatians 6:9*

Genesis 28:15 *Behold, I am with you, and I will watch over you wherever you go, and I will bring you back to this land. I will not leave you until I have done what I have promised.* (NIV)

December 22

YOU WILL NEVER KNOW THE VALUE OF A MOMENT---UNTIL IT BECOMES A MEMORY

Don't take anything for granted. At this moment someone is taking their last breath and would give anything for a few more moments on earth.

You are much more fortunate than you give yourself credit for.

You need to learn to appreciate and be grateful for everything you have. Instead of looking at those who have more than you do, look around and you will see there are many others who are not as fortunate than you.

Unfortunately, you really don't know how good you have it until it's gone. Never take someone you love for granted. Hold that person close to your heart because you might wake up one day and realize you lost a diamond while you were collecting stones.

Hebrews 13:16 *Make sure you don't take things for granted and go slack in working for the common good: share what you have with others.* (MSG)

December 23

COURAGE FOR THE FUTURE

To be courageous means to live with the heart. The way of the heart is the way of courage. It is to live in insecurity, love, trust and move into the unknown.

Most people worry about their future, but the future is yet to come and yet to be. It has a great possibility. It will come and you cannot stop it. Every minute the future is becoming the present and the present is becoming the past.

The present is nothing but a movement into the future. It is a step you have already taken and cannot take back.

You need to focus on the present more. If you are going through a difficult time, pray about it and remember, "This too shall pass."

Matthew 6:34 *Therefore, do not be anxious about tomorrow, for tomorrow will be anxious for itself. (ESV)*

December 24

QUIT BLAMING OTHERS

Quit blaming others for the way your life has turned out. I often hear people saying, "I'm this way because of my parents", or "My husband has made me so bitter and untrusting."

People are so quick to point their finger at everyone else for the way their life has turned out. Stop blaming others, for you are the victim and result of your own circumstances.

You can change your life, if you truly want to. Whenever I start to blame someone else, I remember this wonder Chinese proverb:

He who blames *others* has a long way to go on his journey.
He who blames h*imself* is halfway there.
He who blames *no one* has arrived.

Take responsibility for your life and if you aren't happy, change it.

Romans 2:1 *You, therefore, have no excuse, you who pass judgment on someone else, for at whatever point you judge another, you are condemning yourself, because you who pass judgment do the same things.* (NIV)

December 25

LIFE IS MERELY A JOURNEY

I hope there is days when your coffee tastes like magic, the music makes you dance, strangers make you smile, and the sky tonight touches and warms your soul. I hope you fall in love with being alive again!

Enjoy your life and be thankful for what you have—not what you don't have. There are people who truly love you. Be happy because you are alive and make the world a better place.

It is up to you to be happy. Nobody can do that for you, but you. It is your choice. Take time to do the things that bring a smile to your face and surround yourself with people who you love. We are just visiting here—this is not our final home. Life is a journey—enjoy the trip.

Ecclesiastes 11:9 *You are young, be happy while you are young, and let your heart give you joy in the days of your youth. (NIV)*

December 26

BE THE AWESOME WOMAN GOD CREATED YOU TO BE

Don't let people run your life for you. You can't go through life trying to please everyone else. You can't be worried about what everyone else thinks of you. Whether it's your hair, your figure or your beliefs.

You can't let the judgment of others stop you from being the awesome woman God created you to be. You are unique and one-of-a-kind. There is nobody like you.

You can't let the judgment of others stop you from being you. Because if you do, you will not longer be you---but will be someone everyone else wants you to be!

Jeremiah 1:5 *Before I formed you in the womb I knew you, and before you were born I consecrated you: I appointed you a prophet to the nations.* (NIV)

December 27

DON'T PUT OFF A VISIT

You cannot do a kindness too soon, for you never know how soon it will be too late.

Never put off visiting a family member or friend who you haven't seen for awhile.

And never put off telling a loved one how much they mean to you.

The best part of being with someone you care about is knowing that they know how important they really are.

Tomorrow's life is too late. Live today.

John 3:16 *For God so loved the world that he gave his one and only Son, that whoever believes in him shall not perish. (KJV)*

December 28

STRUGGLES IN LIFE

No matter how much it hurts now, someday you will look back and realize your struggles changed your life for the better. Your personal life and professional life are all intertwined.

Struggle is painful, but it is the most inspirational thing in the world---as long as you treat it that way.

Strength and growth come only through continuous effort and struggle.

Romans 5:3-5 *And not only so, but we glory in tribulations also; knowing that tribulation worketh patience. (KJV)*

December 29

SHAKE IT OFF—LET IT GO

Sometimes the best thing you can do is not think, not wonder, not imagine, and not obsess. Just breathe and have faith that everything will work out for the best.

Letting it all go is not an easy thing to do, but it is something you must learn to do if you want a peaceful life. Being able to let go does not mean to get rid off. To let go means to let be. When we let be with compassion, things come and go on their own.

Ephesians 4:31 *Let all bitterness and wrath and anger and clamor and slander be put away from you, along with malice. (ESV)*

December 30

JESUS IS OUR LIFEGUARD

When you feel like you're drowning in life, don't worry---your lifeguard walks on water! Jesus is our best example of a New Testament lifeguard for He laid down His life for us so that we could pass from the darkness to the Kingdom of God.

He guards our life by telling us that if we want life, what we need to do is to say 'no' to ourselves, pick up our cross every day and follow Him. He shows us how to save our life rather than losing it.

Luke 9:25 *What good will it do you if you win the entire world, but lose or forfeit your own self? (NIV)*

December 31

AN END AND A NEW BEGINNING

Well this is the last day of the year. You made it though yet another one. It may have been trying and stressful at times--but with the grace of God you survived!

Get on your knees and thank God for everything He has done and given you. Ask Him to protect and comfort you in the year to come. Nobody knows when the last day of their life will be, but don't worry about it, for that is when you will go back home to meet your maker. Oh---how glorious that will be!

But until then, while you are still here on earth: Obey and worship Him; pray to Him, and tell others who He is and what He has done for you!

God loves you—His goodness and mercy covers you. Count your blessings and live with gratitude. Make your life an offering of thanks in response to all God has done for you.

Psalm 50:14 *Make thankfulness your sacrifice to God, and keep the vows you made to the Most High. (NLT)*

EPILOGUE

After two long years I finally finished what I consider to be the best book I have ever written. This journey has not been easy, for many unforeseen situations occurred that held me back from completing it. But with the willpower and patience to continue, which God and God alone gave me, I completed the work, for He is, and always will be, my inspiration and guidance.

I hope you enjoy reading the **Whispers From God**, for they are important messages and lessons that He gave me to teach you.

Life is a journey and the world we live in today has continued to deteriorate with ongoing wars, abuse, and the evils of the world. This is because the enemy is constantly trying to distract you from your walk with the Lord.

Be strong and know you are merely visiting here. Life is fleeting and you are one day closer to returning to your Father in your forever home in Heaven.

Victoria

Matthew 24:6 *You will hear of wars and rumors of wars, but see to it that you are not alarmed. Such things must happen, but the end is still to come. (NIV)*

UPLIFTING BIBLE VERSES TO REMEMBER

You Say	God Says	Bible Verses
I Can't Figure It Out	I Will Direct Your Step	Proverbs 3:5-9
I Am Tired	I Will Give You Rest	Matthew 11:28-30
It's Impossible	All Things Are Possible	Luke 18:27
Nobody Loves Me	I Love You	John 3:16
I Can't Forgive Myself	I Forgive You	Romans 8:1
It's Not Worth It	It Will Be Worth It	Romans 8:28
I'm Not Smart Enough	I Will Give You Wisdom	Corinthians 1:30
I'm Not Able	I Am Able	Corinthians 9:8
I Can't Go On	My Grace Is Sufficient	Corinthians 12:9
I Can't Do It	You Can Do All Things	Philippians 4:13
I Can't Manage	I Will Supply All You Need	Philippians 4:19
I Am Afraid	I Have Not Given You Fear	2 Timothy 1:7
I Feel All Alone	I Will Never Leave You	Hebrews 13:5

Printed in the United States
By Bookmasters